D1559198

THE LEBANESE WAR

Yassir Arafat

THE
LEBANESE
WAR

*Its Origins and
Political Dimensions*

by

HARALD VOCKE

ST. MARTIN'S PRESS · NEW YORK

First published in the United Kingdom by
C. Hurst & Co. (Publishers) Ltd.,
1–2 Henrietta Street, London WC2E 8PS

Translated from the German by A. K. H. Weinrich
and Ilse Fisher

Photographs
Frontispiece, 1, 2, 4, 6, 7, *Frankfurter Allgemeine Zeitung*
3, 5, 8, the Lebanese Forces

CONTENTS

Preface   *page* vii

Chapters

   I. The Country   1

  II. Religious Communities in Lebanon   4

 III. Lebanon in Colonial Times   9

 IV. The National Agreement as a Basis for
      Democratic Co-existence   12

  V. Population Figures and Political
     Representation   15

 VI. Successes and Crises of Lebanese Democracy   19

 VII. Voting Blocs and Political Parties   23

VIII. The Palestinian Refugees and the Arab States   31

 IX. The Palestinian Arabs and Lebanon   35

  X. From the Outbreak of the Civil War to the
     Beginning of Sarkis' Presidency   39

 XI. Syrian Peace Troops in Beirut   48

 XII. The Politics of Balance versus Terror   53

XIII. A New Massacre of Christians and the
      Gradual Crumbling of the Armistice   57

XIV. The Lebanese War: Reality and Propaganda   61

     Postscript   68

Appendixes

   I. The Military Forces engaged in the Lebanese
     War (November 1976)   71

  II. Bibliographical Note   76

    Index   78

    Plates   *between pages* 54–55

PREFACE

The civil war in Lebanon produced changes which will affect the future of the entire Near East. New factors of power have emerged, and old, firmly established power groups have sunk into political impotence. Deserted by Europe and the United States, the Lebanese Christians defended themselves against the overwhelming power of their enemies.

The Christians were surprised when they discovered how far their fighting morale and their command of modern weapons surpassed those of their opponents. Adjacent to Israel, a Western-oriented democratic state, and to the Syrian Arab Republic, which still stands at the cross-roads between tradition and progress, between Asiatic despotism and democratic freedom, Christian Lebanon is emerging unexpectedly as a new political factor in the Eastern Mediterranean. In this war, Palestinian guerrillas allied themselves with Right- and Left-radical Lebanese groups and with mercenaries from Libya, Iraq and Somalia, to fight against the Lebanese Christians in the name of *Urubah*, the pan-Arabism which provided a new deity for Arab nationalists who were moving ever further away from traditional Islamic values.

In the last hundred years, the Lebanese Christians have played a leading role in the rebirth of the *Fasih* or 'eloquent' (literary) Arabic language. At the same time they could claim with justice to be the authentic heirs of the old Aramaic cultural values, and to follow in the tradition of the old Syriac religious authors among whom Ephrem the Syrian is still today regarded as the outstanding representative. And were they not also descendants of the brave Phoenicians to whom the Mediterranean cultures owed not only their lettered alphabet but also their first knowledge of Atlantic seafaring? Indeed, the Christians of the Lebanese mountains have little in common with the way of life of the Arabian deserts, whose nomadic tribes shaped the character of Arab culture.

According to a definition of the Baath Arab Socialist Party, an Arab is anyone who speaks the Arabic language and wishes to be an Arab. By this definition, Lebanese

Christians are no longer Arabs as they do not wish to be
counted as such. Many of them even wish to replace literary
Arabic, the language of the Koran and of Islam, by a new
literary language, namely Lebanese, although in the opinion
of Arab Muslims this language is only the crude Arabic
dialect of the people inhabiting the Lebanese mountains and,
as many Muslims believe, unfit for print.

The Christians, certainly, are not responsible for all the
changes to which the results of the Lebanese War may lead
the Near East. During the war, they were mainly concerned
with the defence of their principal settlements. With the
advantage of hindsight it is easier now than two years ago to
discern that the Palestinian guerrillas had planned and
prepared for the war over a long period. And they started the
war at a moment when they believed they could count on a
speedy victory. To the outside world it seemed in the early
months of the war that the Palestinians were playing the role
of uninvolved spectators. But it is now known that the first
wave of attackers who tried to storm the East Beirut
Christian suburb of Ain Rummaneh consisted mainly not of
Lebanese Muslims but of guerrillas belonging to the largest
Palestinian fighting organisation, al Fatah. At the height of
the fighting in 1976, Salah Khalaf, the most influential Fatah
leader, declared that the war aim of the Palestinians was the
conquest of the whole Christian North of Lebanon. This aim
they have been unable to achieve, and moreover they themselves were driven by the Christian militia out of the refugee
camps which they had built up in East Beirut, into for-
tresses—Tell Zaatar, Jisr al Basha and Debeiyeh. Syria
became publicly involved in the civil war for the first time in
the summer of 1976, siding with the Christians, and together
with the Christians was counted among the military victors in
the battles for Beirut.

Israel derived even greater benefit than Syria from the war
unleashed by the Palestinian guerrillas: ever since the
beginning of the Syrian intervention in Lebanon, the most
efficient Syrian fighting units were tied up there, and no
longer threatened the Jewish state.

The so-called Palestine question as such will not be discussed in the following pages. As Near East correspondent of
the German daily newspaper *Frankfurter Allgemeine Zeitung*,
the author in past years has made considerable efforts to ex-

plain to Western readers the tragic fate of the Arabs of Palestine. He still advocates that their case should be considered with sympathy. But when the Palestinian leaders declared that the 'Road to Palestine' should lead via the slopes of the Lebanese mountains, they lost many old friends. Certainly it will be impossible in the future to overlook the consequences of the Lebanese war—and of Palestinian atrocities committed during this war—for the political aspirations of the dispersed Arabs who consider the former British mandated territory of Palestine to be their homeland.

The Christians are today the dominant political power in Lebanon. The Palestinian guerrillas have influence and military strength only in so far as they receive weapons and funds from other Arab countries and from communist states. In Beirut, the Sunni Muslims have almost entirely ceased to play a political role in Lebanon. Even during the war their leaders were forced to surrender all influence to the Palestinians and to the Druze Kemal Jumblatt, at that time spokesmen for the Lebanese Left. With the loss of power of the Sunni, which can be seen in Damascus also, the old form of co-existence between Christians and Muslims, reflected in the Lebanese national pact of 1943, had come to an end.

The future is uncertain. Only one thing is sure: namely, that no solution of the problems raised by the civil war will be possible without the leaders of those Christians who fought in the war being heard. The Christians will only be satisfied with a complete internal restructuring of the country. If this is not understood by President Sarkis—who, although a Christian, is more sympathetic towards the Lebanese Muslims and the Palestinian guerrillas than towards his co-religionists—his political programme will be wrecked.

In spite of the significance of Lebanon in the West's relations with other Arab states of the Near East, little about this small, ancient country is known at present in the West. This account was begun when the civil war was at its height, and was published in German at the end of 1976.* Its favourable reception among politicians and journalists in German-speaking countries encouraged the undertaking of this English edition, which, because of the passing of time, appears in an expanded form. The brief survey it presents of

---

* *Was geschah im Libanon?*

the most important religious communities and population groups in Lebanon and of the country's recent history may be helpful to those who are not closely familiar with the situation in the Near East. These notes end with a critical analysis of the propaganda of the Palestinian guerrillas; for this propaganda has misled several Western observers of the Lebanese war.

The truth about the Lebanese war is different from the reports published by many Western newspaper and television stations during the last two years. When the Christians in Lebanon were fighting for their survival, cut off from the outside world by having no news connections, hardly any voice was heard other than that of their opponents. There was never a 'Falange' of Right-wing Christians attacking 'progressive Muslims' in Lebanon, as many reports from Beirut, inspired by Palestinian sources, pretended. The following pages are written to correct this distorted picture.

Frankfurt am Main,
October 1977

I

THE COUNTRY

The territory of the republic of Lebanon, together with the Republic of Syria, the Hashemite Kingdom of Jordan and the state of Israel, belong to that part of Asia Minor which was still known in the last century by the collective name 'Syria'. Ever since antiquity, Lebanon's fate has been closely connected with the development of its territorial neighbours. But in character the Lebanese mountains, with their snow-covered peaks, and the fertile Mediterranean coast, are very different from the more desert-like region which comprises present-day Syria and its southern neighbour, the Biblical Palestine.

Lebanon is divided geographically into four distinct zones: a small coastal strip along the Mediterranean borders on the precipitous Lebanon Mountains which run from north to south and fall on the east side to the fertile high plateau of Bekaa. The Anti-Lebanon Mountains form the eastern boundary of both the Bekaa plain and the Lebanese national territory. With its 10,400 square kilometres Lebanon is half the size of Wales and Monmouth.

The most important towns in Lebanon are situated along the Mediterranean coastline. Apart from the capital Beirut, the towns are, from south to north, Tyre, Sidon, Jouniyeh, Jubail, Batroun and Tripoli. Under Phoenician rule, the coastal region already flourished remarkably in the second millennium B.C. The ancient Phoenician city-states grew rich through their long-haul trade and through the export of purple dye obtained from the purple snail. In Jubail (the Byblos of antiquity), Sidon (Saida) and Tyre (Sur), as well as in Beirut, impressive ruins still bear witness to ancient glory. In early antiquity Phoenicia comprised only the coastal region adjoining the western slopes of the Lebanon mountains, but the Romans sometimes used the term 'Phoenicia' to include also the whole Western part of Syria, with Damascus and Emesa, known today as Homs.

1

The Semitic peoples and European civilisation owe their alphabet to the Phoenicians. The Phoenician religion, with its male god Baal and a mother-goddess, was closely related to the beliefs of the neighbouring Semitic peoples. However, some Phoenician mythological figures, like the beautiful Adonis who was torn to pieces by a boar, and Europa who was abducted to Crete by a bull, stimulated the imagination of the Greeks and Romans. In the ancient myth, Europa, who gave her name to our continent and its culture, was a daughter of the King of Tyre which had once been the principal Phoenician town on the Mediterranean. The most important Phoenician colony in the Western Mediterranean was Carthage, which under Hannibal became Rome's great enemy.

Pride in their Phoenician heritage is an essential element in the national consciousness of the present-day Lebanese. Their national character has been no less decisively formed by the Lebanon Mountains. These mountains have the highest winter rainfall in the Near East, and rivers flow down their sides through green valleys into the Mediterranean. The Eastern slopes of the mountains are drier and thus have less vegetation. The highest peak in the range is Qornet es Saouda in the north, 3,090 metres high; from this point the mountain range decreases in height towards the south; the Sannin peak east of Beirut is 2,630 metres high and Jebel Niha, east of Saida, only 1,860 metres.

The broad characteristics of the Lebanon Mountains are easy to take in, but the multiplicity of peaks, high plateaux, river valleys and smaller mountains in this imposing *massif* on which the snow continues to lie right into the hottest summer months, make a complex picture. In the coastal plain they grow oranges, bananas and vegetables, and in the uplands apples, cherries, figs and vines. Since antiquity, peasants have tried to expand the agricultural land at their disposal by terrace cultivation.

To the east of the Lebanon Mountains the fertile Bekaa plateau runs parallel to it, with the Anti-Lebanon Mountains on its east side—the plain is 20 kilometres broad. The frontier crosses the highest point of the Hermon mountains (2,800 metres), which are a continuation of the Anti-Lebanon to the south. While the Bekaa plateau, with its rich wheat fields and vineyards, has a resemblance to Southern Europe, the rugged Anti-Lebanon peaks and the adjoining Hermel region in the north show desert characteristics. Both the Lebanese Mediterranean coast and the Bekaa valley have served, ever since antiquity, as main roads for conquerors and as trade routes for caravans travelling from Egypt and Palestine to Northern Syria, or from the north into Palestine.

II
RELIGIOUS COMMUNITIES IN LEBANON

Since the early Middle Ages the country's mountain valleys have been places of refuge for persecuted religious minorities. At first sight, the multiplicity of religious communities appears confusing; some Lebanese authorities count eighteen different denominations. However, the religious communities which are significant in the political life of the country are not difficult to grasp. They belong to three major religions: Christianity, Islam and the Druze faith.

The four most important Christian communities are the Maronites, the Greek Orthodox, the Greek Catholics (Melkites) and the Gregorian (Orthodox) Armenians. The Muslims in Lebanon are divided into Sunnites and Shiites. A third religious community, independent of both Islam and Christianity, consists of the followers of the post-Islamic sect of Druzes.

About two-thirds of the Lebanese Christians are Maronites. As early as 1854, the great German geographer Carl Ritter gave a description of the Maronites which remains a classic: 'an athletic, handsome people, full of intelligence, courage and enterprise, and on the same footing as those Arab tribes which have not yet declined. They are industrious and quite the opposite of the Turkish fanatics. They speak Arabic, not Turkish; they live by means of agriculture in the Lebanon Mountains, and have been successful in remaining independent from Turkish domination throughout many centuries by courageous defence of their mountain possessions.' After the Syrian persecution of Christians in 1860, Pope Leo XIII called them *rosa inter spinas* (a rose among thorns). These oriental Christians derive their name from St. Maron, a 4th-century hermit who lived in north-eastern Syria. He was buried in the valley of the Orontes river near the ancient Apamea, and for several centuries a monastery named after him flourished there. However, it is said to have been John Maron, a monk from Antioch, who brought the

4

Maronites to the high valleys of Northern Lebanon in the
seventh century. The influx of persecuted Maronite Christians from Syria into the Lebanon Mountains continued into
the ninth century. In the Crusades the Maronites fought
alongside the Crusaders and united themselves with the
Roman Catholic Church, but they retained their own liturgy
and their own religious leader, the Maronite 'Patriarch of
Antioch and of the whole Orient', whose residence is always
in Lebanon.

Western writers are sceptical about the claim of Maronite
authors that their church has always been united with Rome
since the time of St. Maron. Still, the fact remains that since
the Middle Ages the Maronite Church has been the greatest
and most important of all the oriental churches that are
united with Rome. In the political field, the Maronites are
strong supporters of Lebanese independence from the neighbouring Muslim countries.

Traditionally, the Greek Orthodox in Lebanon are closely
linked with other Greek Orthodox Christians of the ancient
ecclesiastical province of Syria; their patriarch resides in
Damascus. Greek Orthodox Arabs have constantly striven for
good relations with Muslim rulers—first with the Caliphs and
Sultans and in recent times with the Arab heads of state.

Members of this community in Lebanon do not regard
themselves as a minority oppressed by neighbouring Muslim
states, but as Arab Christians—as well as being inheritors of
the traditions of the Byzantine empire. In Lebanon—and in
Syria and Palestine—members of this church have been the
intellectual leaders of the Arab left and of the Communist
parties during the last decades. The Orthodox church of the
Soviet Union has revived the close links of tsarist Russia with
the Greek Orthodox church of the Arab Near East, and in
recent decades the Patriarch of Moscow has repeatedly sent
delegations to Beirut. In contrast to the Maronites, who live
predominantly in the valleys of the Lebanon Mountains, the
Greek Orthodox in Lebanon live mainly in Beirut, in the
hinterland of the northern port of Tripoli, and in the South
Lebanon region of Marjayoun.

The Greek Catholic Christians (Melkites) are the second
largest Catholic community. Only at the beginning of the
eighteenth century did they recognise the supremacy of the
Pope and so set themselves apart from the Greek Orthodox

church of the Arab Near East. Because of their link with
Rome, the Melkites are closer to the West than their
Orthodox fellow-Christians. Their Patriarch resides alter-
nately in Damascus, Cairo and Lebanon. The southern towns
of Sidon and Tyre, the town of Zahle in the Western Bekaa
valley, and the province of Shouf in the central high plateau,
are densely populated by Melkites.

The Armenians arrived in Lebanon in large numbers only
in the 1920s, when they were fleeing from persecution and
massacres in their homeland in Asia Minor. They are divided
into Gregorian (Orthodox) Armenians, Armenian Catholics
and Armenian Protestants. More than three-quarters of the
Armenians in Lebanon are members of the Orthodox
Armenian church named after Gregory the Illuminator. The
Armenians are clearly distinguished from the other Lebanese
Christian communities on account of their language and
culture which they have preserved in their new country.

The small minorities of Syrian Orthodox, Syrian Catholics,
Nestorians and Chaldaeans, Latin Catholics and Protestants—in all only 2 per cent of the Lebanese
population—have hardly any political influence.

The Sunni Muslims are named after the *Sunna*, the
transmitted words and deeds of Muhammad. In the modern
Lebanese republic, as in the former Ottoman empire, they
always regarded themselves, before anything else, as members of the worldwide community of Sunni Muslims, and in
their view this means that they belong to the largest and only
orthodox religious community within Islam. In the Lebanese
uplands, which were originally occupied by Maronites and
Druzes, Sunni influence is still minor. The Sunni are con-
centrated on the coast in the cities of Beirut, Tripoli and
Sidon. There are close links of kinship between them and
many Sunni families in neighbouring Syria, especially in
Damascus. The senior representative of the Sunni Muslims in
Lebanon is the Mufti of the republic. He receives his salary
from the state, as do most of the other dignitaries of the
Muslim faith.

Hatred has existed between the Shiite Muslims and the
Sunni ever since the early days of Islam, when *Shiat Ali*, the
party of Ali, was persecuted by the Sunni. The Shiites
recognise only Ali, the nephew and son-in-law of Muhammad, as the Prophet's legitimate heir, but not the Califs Abu

Bakr, Omar and Osman, who were elected by the Muslims after Muhammad's death. The various communities and sects of the Shiites venerate—besides Muhammad, the Prophet of Islam—Ali, Ali's sons Hassan and Hussain, and their descendants. Every year in the Muslim lunar month of Muharram the Shiites commemorate the passion and martyrdom which Hussain suffered in 680 at Kerbela in southern Iraq. In Lebanon the Shiites are the poorest of the religious communities. The majority live in the south and in the Bekaa valley. Only since the 1960s has the Imam of the Shiite Muslims in Lebanon been recognised by the state as the community's spiritual head.

The faith of the Druzes is post-Islamic and secret. This means that the religion came into existence through Islamic influence, but no longer belongs to Islam. The spiritual leaders of the Druzes keep the essential teachings of the faith secret. However, through Druze writings which reached Europe in the last century, their teaching is known to Western oriental scholarship. The Shiite Calif al Hakim bi'amrillah, who died insane in Cairo in 1021, is venerated by the Druzes as a reincarnation of God. Also, in contrast to the Muslims, the Druzes believe in the transmigration of souls. Since the Middle Ages, the 'gate of faith' has been closed: nobody except the children of Druzes can become a Druze. The religious community consists of a small group of initiated 'with knowledge'—the *Uqqal*—and the great mass of those 'without knowledge'—the *Juhhal*. The art of deception, if practised in the interests of the faith, is considered praiseworthy.

Immediately after the foundation of the Druze sect, its followers had to flee from Egypt because of Muslim persecution. After an intense burst of missionary activity in Syria, the Druzes found a new home in the valleys of Southern Lebanon. For centuries the Druze nobles were the political leaders of the independent peasant tribes in the Lebanon Mountains, and until the nineteenth century most of them allied themselves with the Maronite Christians. Since the seventeenth century several renowned Lebanese Druze leaders have been converted to Christianity.

The most notable ruler of the Druzes in Lebanese history, the Emir Fakhreddin II (ruled 1598–1635), was befriended by the Medici Grand Duke Ferdinand I of Tuscany and lived for some time as a guest of the Medici in Florence. Fakhreddin II worked for a close co-operation between the Druzes, the Maronites and the Muslims in Lebanon: he wanted them to stand together for the autonomy of the mountain region in face of claims to domination by the Ottoman Turks. Finally this Druze Emir, the first in modern times to establish closer links between Lebanon and Europe, was defeated in battle by the Ottomans and executed in Constantinople. Today's Lebanese—Christians, Muslims and Druzes alike—regard him as a national hero, a William Tell of the 'Switzerland of the Near East'. Most Druzes live as peasants in the mountains of the central province of Shuf.

Before the outbreak of the civil war, some 6,000 Sephardic Jews are said to have lived in Lebanon, but they have maintained no contact with the neighbouring state of Israel. In times of political crisis, the Lebanese army has protected their homes. In recent decades, these Jews have not been able to exert any significant influence on the political and economic life of Lebanon.

III
LEBANON IN COLONIAL TIMES

Modern Egyptian as well as Lebanese history begins with Napoleon's Eastern campaign in 1798–9. It is true that Napoleon withdrew to Egypt after raising an unsuccessful siege at Acre, which is close to Lebanon's southern border, and that the Lebanese Emir Beshir II maintained a cautious neutrality towards him. Nevertheless, Napoleon ended the medieval rule of the Mamelukes in Egypt, and so made possible the rise of Muhammad Ali. This adventurer of Albanian stock, whose dynasty reigned in Cairo until 1952, subjected the whole of Syria, Lebanon and Palestine to his rule. Under Egyptian sovereignty Beshir II created the first modern administration in Lebanon, but had to flee to Egypt as an exile in 1840 when the European powers forced Egyptian troops to withdrew from Syria.

During the following decades it was mainly external influences that determined the political development of Lebanon. Officially the country continued to be part of the Ottoman empire, as it had been since the conquest of Syria by Selim I in 1516, but the rival European powers constantly intervened in its internal affairs. France continued its role as protecting power of the Catholic Christians of the Ottoman empire, which it had assumed in the sixteenth century under François I. Above all, it maintained close relationships, therefore, with the Maronites. England tried for decades to strengthen the "sick man of Europe", namely the Turkish Ottoman empire, against Russian expansionism. In Lebanon, it was England's Eastern policy to collaborate above all with the Druze leaders. The tsarist empire came forward as the guardian of the Greek Orthodox in the empire.

Already under Beshir II the good relationship which had previously existed between the Maronites and the Druzes disintegrated. In 1843 the Ottomans placed the Lebanon Mountains simultaneously under a Maronite and a Druze *kaimakam* (literally caretaker). The two *kaimakams* administered the Lebanon Mountains as an autonomous region; in the northern part of the range, an area almost exclusively inhabited by Maronites, a Maronite acted as *kaimakam*, while in the southern part of Lebanon, where the majority of the Druzes lived, the post was held by a Druze. Both governors were appointed by the Turkish Pasha, who resided in Sidon.

In 1859 a peasant uprising, which began in the north of Lebanon as a rebellion of Maronite peasants against the great Christian noble families, spread to the south of the country. There the rebellion changed its character, for the Druze peasants, who were obedient to the heads of their feudal families, turned against the Maronite Christians. In 1860 Druze armed bands besieged the Christians in the rural towns of Zahle, Sidon, Hasbaiya and Deir al Qamar and murdered thousands of defenceless Christians, while the Ottoman occupation troops stood by in silence. In August 1860 some 8,000 French soldiers landed in Beirut and pursued the Druze warriors into the southern mountain region and right into the Bekaa valley. The main forces of Druzes thereupon evaded the French by crossing the Anti-Lebanon into the South Syrian 'Druze Mountains'.

At this point an international commission was set up with representatives of five European powers—England, France, Austria, Prussia and Russia—and Turkey. The Lebanon Mountains were declared an autonomous region, administered by a Christian *mutasarrif*, or governor, directly responsible to the government in Constantinople. The autonomous region administered by the *mutasarrif* included only the territory later called 'Little Lebanon', i.e. the Lebanon Mountains themselves without the important ports of Tripoli, Beirut and Sidon; a total of only 5,740 square kilometres, hardly more than half the size of the later 'Greater Lebanon', which became the modern republic. During the summer months the seat of the Turkish governor was in the old Druze castle, Beiteddin, in the South Lebanese mountains, while in winter it was in the rural town of Baabda, 10 kilometres south of Beirut. During the First World War, Lebanon was subject to Turkish military government. A famine in the mountain villages, which were blockaded by the Turks, caused many deaths.

After the conquest of Palestine and Syria by British troops under General Allenby and the Arab troops of the Hashemite Emir Faisal, the conference of San Remo in April 1920 declared Syria and Lebanon to be French mandated territories. At Khan Maissalun in the Anti-Lebanon French troops inflicted a devastating defeat on the army of Faisal, who had himself proclaimed king of Greater Syria at Damascus in March 1920. In July 1920 the French occupied Damascus, and on 31 August the same year the French mandatory power announced the unification of the Bekaa valley, the Anti-Lebanon and the Lebanese Mediterranean coast with the former Lebanon mountain region. This new 'Greater Lebanon' was larger than the territory occupied predominantly by Lebanese Christians, but smaller than that formerly controlled by Fakhreddin II and Beshir II.

Under the French mandate, yet with the co-operation of Lebanese jurists, the republic of Lebanon received in 1926 a modern constitution on the European model. After the fall of France in the Second World War, Lebanon came under the control of the pro-Hitler Vichy government. This was in 1940–1. However, after the invasion of Lebanon and Syria by British and French troops, General de Gaulle visited Beirut. On 26 November 1941, in the name of de Gaulle's government-in-exile, General Catroux declared Lebanon an independent country.

In September 1943, parliamentary elections took place and the Lebanese cabinet chose the Maronite Beshara al Khoury as head of state. President Khoury appointed the Sunni Muslim Riad al Solh Prime Minister. The Solh government suspended in the Lebanese constitution all articles which in the past had given special privileges to the former mandatory power and its high commissioner in Lebanon. Thereupon the French arrested President Khoury, the Prime Minister Solh, and several members of the cabinet, and detained them in a fortress in the eastern rural town of Rashaya. Indignation and unrest immediately swept through all the religious communities, and under pressure from the United States, England and the Arab countries, France freed the prisoners of Rashaya on 22 November. Beshara al Khoury resumed the office of President. The Lebanese now regard this date, 22 November 1943, as marking their country's political independence.

IV

THE NATIONAL AGREEMENT AS A BASIS FOR DEMOCRATIC CO-EXISTENCE

Christians on the one hand, and Muslims and Druzes on the other, attach different values to the notions of state, nation and democracy. To the Muslims and Druzes these concepts are alien. Modern parliamentary democracy derives from the ancient Graeco-Roman teachings of the state, but it has been created anew in the Christian cultures of Western Europe. The concepts of state and nation, as used in modern Western languages, are also linked to Christian culture. For Christians the division between state and religion constitutes no fundamental contradiction; they recognise that within the national boundaries which have assumed their present form through the forces of history, a nation exists of which all the citizens have equal rights.

To the Muslim who takes his religion seriously, the nation is first of all the *umma*, also called *ummat Muhammad*, i.e. the community of all Muslims all over the world. A state which is not governed according to Islamic law is, for the believing Muslim, at best a necessary evil. Solidarity among Muslims of different nationalities is given a higher value than loyalty to a non-Islamic state. Separation between state and religion is not permissible. Muslims believe that God has revealed in the Koran the only valid world order, and that he did this in the Arabic language and in every detail. Besides this, the sayings (*hadith*, pl. *ahadith*) and deeds of the Prophet Muhammad will always have for Muslims an exemplary force. In the regulation of all questions concerning political life and civil rights, the Koran and the *hadith* are the supreme guide. Modern parliamentary democracy is therefore irreconcilable with the spirit of Islam. According to Islamic law, the relationships between Muslims and non-Muslims are regulated in no spirit of equality. Only Muslims are full citizens and all others are subjects, who have to be simultaneously tolerated and protected. Whereas during

12

'Holy War' the duty of a Muslim is to convert or kill idolaters, he offers to Christians and Jews, as 'peoples of the Book', the possibility of a permanent subjection under the Islamic state/As '*ahl al dhimma*' ('protected community'), Christians and Jews were already, under the first Caliphs, allowed to keep their own religions. But they had to pay special taxes to the victorious Muslims. They could not serve in the army, or carry arms. Muslims might take Christian and Jewish wives, but Christians and Jews could not marry Muslim women. *Dhimmis* had to distinguish themselves from Muslims by means of a special form of dress, their houses could not be taller than those of Muslims, and they were not allowed to ride on horseback. In their religious observance they had to avoid all ostentation, such as processions and the ringing of church bells.

Under the Ottoman empire, the non-Islamic religious communities were subject as autonomous bodies to an Ottoman Sultan who, as spiritual head of the Muslims, was called Caliph. The Sublime Porte first recognised the Greek Orthodox patriarch in Constantinople as spiritual head of all Christians in the empire, but later the Ottoman rulers also recognised other Christian churches, including the Maronites and Melkites, as independent religious communities.

For the oriental Christians their religious communities, called *millet* in the Turkish language, were their only true political home. At the time when modern nationalism developed in Europe, the different *millets* in the Ottoman empire began to emphasise their own distinct character in relation both to each other and to their Muslim environment. People began to equate the Turkish word *millet*, which was borrowed from Arabic, with the Western concept of 'nation'. In Lebanon it was above all the Maronites who began to regard themselves as a nation in their own right.

In the Lebanon Mountains the Christians had never been subject to the severe restrictions which Islamic law imposed on all *dhimmis*: 'The Christians in Lebanon were subject to no restrictions in the exercise of their religion; they dressed as they liked and rode on horseback like their neighbours, the Druzes. Outward signs of discrimination were practically non-existent in Lebanon' (Wilhelm Kewening, *Die Koexistens der Religionsgemeinschaften im Libanon*, Berlin, 1965).

The Druze community was not regarded as a true *millet* in the Ottoman empire. The Druzes saw themselves as a chosen people. Their secret religion, however, induced them to adjust themselves opportunistically to the most powerful force with which they had to deal. Whereas in the seventeenth and eighteenth centuries leading Druzes openly accepted Christianity, in recent times Lebanese Druzes have tended strongly to claim to be Muslims.

The independent republic of Lebanon decided, right from its inception, to adopt a democratic form of government. To this end the religious communities formed a compromise, the unsigned 'Lebanese National Pact'. It was adopted in October 1943 by the Maronite President Beshara al-Khoury, representing the Lebanese Christians, and by the Sunni Prime Minister Riad al Solh, representing the Lebanese Muslims and Druzes. All religious communities recognised their duty to guarantee together the country's independence. The Christians specifically renounced their traditional policy of calling upon European states, in particular France, to act as protecting powers *vis-à-vis* the political ambitions of the Muslims. The Muslims, for their part, agreed that they would no longer call on other Islamic states to intervene in the internal affairs of the country. Within the Lebanese state the religious communities agreed to preserve the current *status quo*, the existing balance of power. It was also agreed that the Lebanese President should always be a Maronite Christian, the speaker of the parliament a Shiite Muslim, and the Prime Minister a Sunni Muslim.

V
POPULATION FIGURES AND
POLITICAL REPRESENTATION

The last official census in Lebanon was taken in 1932. Its findings distinguished between the number of Lebanese living in Lebanon at the time and the total number of Lebanese citizens, including those living in foreign countries. Since the last century, it has been mainly the Christians who have left Lebanon to find new homes as immigrants in Latin America, North America, Egypt or West Africa, or who spend some time abroad so as to earn money and then return home with their savings. Muslims and Druzes leave Lebanon far less frequently than do Christians.

The distribution of parliamentary seats among the denominations is based on the returns of the 1932 census, taking into account all Lebanese citizens including those living abroad. Already then, the majority of Lebanese living abroad had surrendered their Lebanese citizenship. The first parliament of the independent republic had fifty-five seats, and the parliament elected in 1972 had ninety-nine seats. The proportion of six parliamentary seats for Christians to five for Muslims and Druzes has always been retained.

Since 1932, only estimates of the population have been published, based on the official birth and death registration. The estimate for 1956 showed that in the total population of 1,411,416, the proportion of Christians had slightly increased; according to these calculations, some 54 per cent of the population were Christians and 44 per cent Muslims and Druzes. The birth-rate is believed to be much higher among Muslims than among Christians, but during the 1950s the infant mortality rate among Christians had declined more rapidly than among the Muslims and Druzes. During the 1960s the statistical office of the republic published only total population estimates, which were not subdivided according to religious communities. This was because the leaders of both the Christians and the Muslims feared that the publication of proportional changes in the relationship between the religious

THE 1932 CENSUS AND PARLIAMENTARY REPRESENTATION OF THE DENOMINATIONS

Religious Community	Excluding Foreign Lebanese	Including Lebanese Citizens abroad	% of Total Population	No. of Parliamentary Seats 1960–76
Maronites	227,000	261,043	30	30
Greek Orthodox	77,312	90,275	10	11
Greek Catholics (Melkites)	46,709	52,602	6	6
Armenians (Orthodox, Catholics and Protestants)	21,992	34,296	4	5
Sunni	178,130	182,842	21	20
Shiites	155,035	158,425	18	19
Druzes	53,334	56,812	6·5	6
Others*	23,114	24,534	3	2
Total	782,626	860,829	98·5	99

* Smaller Christian communities and Jews

communities might cause political unrest. For 1969 the statistical office announced that a total of 2,667,427 persons were registered as nationals.

Such figures give the impression of a degree of accuracy which is in fact unobtainable without a new census. It is estimated that in 1975, before the outbreak of the civil war, there were more than 3 million Lebanese citizens. The question of which direction the relationship between the religious groupings has taken since 1932 is hotly debated. A new census can only be carried out several years after the end of the civil war, and in the absence of such a new census no pronouncement on a change in the relative sizes of the religious communities can be other than speculative.

In the following section some general points will be raised which are often ignored in discussions of power distribution between the Christians and the Muslims, and it is hoped that these will contribute to a better understanding of the situation.

In every parliamentary democracy the right to vote is tied to citizenship. Hence Lebanese living abroad who have retained their citizenship must be counted as representative of their religious communities. On the other hand, people who live in Lebanon as 'guest-workers', tourists, illegal immigrants or refugees and who have not been granted Lebanese citizenship will not be included. Before the civil war, at least 500,000 Syrian guest-workers were living in Lebanon, as well as the following, most of whom were illegal immigrants: Syrian Orthodox Christians from south-eastern Turkey; Kurds from Syria, Iraq and Turkey; Christians of different denominations who had fled from northern Iraq to Beirut during the Kurdish war; and members of radical political parties, especially from Syria, Jordan, Iraq and Egypt, who sought refuge in Lebanon in order to escape political persecution at home or to engage in political activity unimpeded.

The group of non-Lebanese who are most active politically are the Palestinian refugees—either those who found refuge in Lebanon after the Arab–Israeli war of 1948–9, or those who have been born there of refugee parents.

According to reliable estimates, at least 1,000,000 non-Lebanese were living in the country when the civil war broke out. Lebanon is the only state in the history of the Arab Near East which has realised equal co-existence between Christians and Muslims. Because the National Pact allocated the office of President to a Christian, Lebanon is different from all other Arab states, in whose constitutions the office of President is reserved for a Muslim. The Lebanese Maronites fear that, should the Beirut parliament have a majority of non-Christian representatives, the status of Christians in Lebanon might become like that of Christians in the other Arab states. Lebanese Christians might then find their legal position reduced to an inferior level—similar, for example, to that of Coptic Christians in Egypt who exercise no real influence in their country's politics, although they are far more numerous than the *total* population of Lebanon. A new distribution of power, which would deprive the Lebanese Christians of the office of President, would also destroy the foundation of the National Pact of 1943. The Maronites agree that the present distribution of parliamentary seats does not correspond with the strength of the different religious communities, but they point out that in the mountain regions they are still in the majority. In case a revival of Lebanese democracy within a centralised unitary state should prove to be no longer possible, the Maronites propose a new state model for discussion: that of a federation with separate administrations for the Christians on the one hand, and for the Muslims and Druzes on the other.

Until the civil war not only the parliamentary seats but also the most important posts in the civil service were distributed among the religious communities according to their denominational proportion. Muslim politicians allege that in this respect Muslims and Druzes have been placed at a disadvantage. However the Maronites argue that denominationalism has worked to the advantage of the Muslims, because the better educational standard of Lebanese Christians would have given Christians a much larger proportion of civil service posts, if these had been allocated solely by merit.

According to Ministry of Education figures, about 50 per cent of all Lebanese were illiterate in 1958. The proportions of those who could neither read nor write among the various religious communities were as follows:

	% illiterate
Shiite Muslims	79
Sunni Muslims	59
Druzes	51
Greek Orthodox	50
Maronites	42
Melkites	31

VI

SUCCESSES AND CRISES OF
LEBANESE DEMOCRACY

The history of the independent republic of Lebanon begins in
the atmosphere of trust and co-operation which existed
between an outstanding Christian politician, the Maronite
President Beshara al-Khoury, and the most outstanding
Lebanese Muslim of modern times, the Sunni Prime Minister
Riad al-Solh. These two politicians pursued a common
political goal which is well expressed by their key-phrase
'Lebanon—neither Occident nor Orient'. Lebanon participated in the first Arab–Israeli war with its own troops
under the command of General Fuad Chehab, who later
became President. In March 1949, on the island of Rhodes,
the Lebanese and Israelis negotiated a ceasefire, which was
countersigned at the Lebanese–Israeli border by the military
leaders on 23 March 1949. On 15 July 1951, Riad al-Solh
was shot dead in the Jordanian capital, Amman, by a
member of the extreme Right-wing 'Syrian National
Socialist' party.

After nine years as President, Beshara al-Khoury was
succeeded in the autumn of 1952 by the Maronite Camille
Chamoun. Under the liberal-democratic Chamoun, voting
rights were extended to women. Chamoun's main opponent
was the Egyptian President Abdul Nasser, who gained a
strong following through his appeals to pan-Arab sentiment
among both Muslims and Christians in Lebanon. To protect
Lebanon against the aggressive policies of Nasser and the
Soviet Union, which under Khrushchev began to support the
radical Arab nationalists in the Middle East, the country
became a subscriber to the Eisenhower Doctrine. Through
this move it won American economic support and the right to
ask for American military assistance in times of political
crisis. The membership declaration of the Eisenhower
Doctrine was formally ratified by the Lebanese parliament in
April 1957.

On 1 February 1958 Syria joined with Egypt in a 'United

Arab Republic'. More than 100,000 Lebanese poured into Syria to see Nasser, who, from Damascus, appealed to the Lebanese people to force their government to break with the West; in its foreign policy Lebanon should follow the same course as the 'United Arab Republic'. On 8 May 1958 the Lebanese publisher Nassib Metni, an opponent of Chamoun, was assassinated in Beirut by unknown killers who were never traced. The opinion is prevalent in Beirut that Egypt instigated the assassination in order to arouse the passions of Chamoun's opponents. Nasser, who was on a visit to the Soviet Union, sent his message of condolence to Beirut from Stalingrad. This message contained the words 'Metni died a hero'. At the same time Nasser threatened to take up residence in Damascus during the ensuing months 'to keep a close watch on the situation in Lebanon'.

The death of Metni was immediately followed by uprisings all over Lebanon. Armed followers of Nasser barricaded themselves in the Beirut Muslim quarter, Basta. During the crisis, which resembled a civil war and lasted till the autumn of 1958, the country was split into two camps: followers of Nasser and Chamoun loyalists. In the Nasser camp were found also leading Sunni Muslims like Saeb Salam from Beirut and Rashid Karame from Tripoli; Shiite Muslims like Sabri Hamade who, as feudal lord, controlled the main region producing hashish (marijuana) in the north of Bekaa valley; the Druze leader Kamal Jumblatt; and well-known Maronite Christians, such as the brothers Hamid and Sulaiman Franjiya from the North Lebanese high plateau and the jurist Fuad Amoun, who were opposed to Chamoun due to personal rivalry in Lebanese politics. The Maronite Patriarch, Me'ushi, who in 1955, contrary to tradition, was not elected to his ecclesiastical dignity by the Lebanese bishops but directly appointed by the Vatican, also sided at first with the Nasserites. The most important supporter of Chamoun in this conflict was the leader of the social democratic Kataeb party, Pierre Gemayel. The Minister of Defence, General Fuad Chehab, at first remained neutral and, together with the army, withdrew himself almost totally from the control of the government. The insurgents were provided with arms by the Syrian province of the 'United Arab Republic'. At the request of Sweden, the United Nations sent observers to the eastern region of the country, and after several weeks this delegation, which included officers of thirteen countries, reached a conclusion which baffled all parties: it could not prove that any delivery of arms or any infiltration from Syria into the Lebanon had taken place. This, at least, was the message of the delegation's official report.

On 14 July 1958 the Hashemite monarchy of Iraq fell through a *coup* staged by young officers. At the request of President Chamoun the United States sent an expeditionary force to Lebanon to meet their obligation to support their ally under the Eisenhower Doctrine. At the same time Britain, at the request of King Hussein, sent air force units to Jordan to support the Hashemite throne in Amman. Nasser went first to Moscow and from there to Damascus. He let troops of the 'United Arab Republic' march to the Lebanese border.

American Near Eastern diplomacy values good relations with Egypt, and therefore during July a compromise was decided upon; it was hoped in this way to find a peaceful settlement of the Lebanon crisis. The American diplomat Robert Murphy negotiated in Lebanon with the leading opponents of Chamoun, namely the Maronite Patriarch Me'ushi, the conservative Maronite party leader Raymond Eddé and the Druze leader Jumblatt. As a result, Nasser stopped his propaganda campaign against American Near Eastern policy. On 31 July 1958 the Lebanese parliament elected the Minister of Defence, Fuad Chehab, as the new President by a large majority. Chehab entered office on 24 September 1958.

Under the presidency of Chehab (1958–64) and later that of Charles Hélou (1964–70), Lebanon followed a neutral course in wider world politics. Yet its policy was marked by a conscious consideration of Egypt's pro-Soviet policies. Until the late 1960s the United States favoured the opponents of Chamoun, their former ally, and many important professorial chairs at the American University in Beirut were filled by representatives of the Arab Left.

On 16 May 1966 Egyptian secret service agents assassinated the journalist Kamil Mruwweh in Beirut. His daily newspaper, *Al Hayat,* was the only Arabic newspaper in Beirut which had regularly given knowledgeable and critical analyses of Egyptian–Soviet Near Eastern policies. The murderers were found, and Gemayel, leader of the Kataeb

Party, used his power as Minister of the Interior to insist on an investigation. At that time he was the only member of the Lebanese cabinet who still dared to criticise openly the constant interference by the Egyptian secret police in the country's affairs.

In the 1960s the premiership was repeatedly held by the North Lebanese Muslim Rashid Karame, who supported the policies of Nasser and the radical demands of the Palestinian leader Ahmed Shukairi. During the Arab-Israeli Six-Day War in June 1967, Lebanon remained neutral. In the later 1960s, the country was enjoying a significant economic boom as the banking centre of the Arab Near East. At the same time, however, its inner stability was constantly being disturbed by radical groups. Alongside the traditional Lebanese power groups, armed Palestinian guerrilla organisations were emerging more and more openly as new factors of political power.

VII

VOTING BLOCS AND POLITICAL PARTIES

The Lebanese voting system is not conducive to the formation of strong democratic parties. This is because, at parliamentary elections, every candidate has to win the votes of many members of alien religious communities in his own electoral district. For example, in the central Lebanese electoral district of Aley, two parliamentary seats are allocated to Maronites, two to Druzes and one to a Greek Orthodox candidate. Every voter in Aley has five votes and with these he must vote for two Maronites, two Druzes and one Greek Orthodox. This means that he may not cast his votes only in favour of candidates of his own denomination. Because of the strong influence which religious affiliations still exert on political life, it is rare in any one electoral district for candidates of the same party to be found on a common electoral roll. On the other hand, it is customary for politicians who are well disposed towards one another but who belong to different parties or prefer to remain independent, to unite in loose alliances as opportunities present themselves, or to join in common electoral rolls or voting blocs.

The voting bloc of the Sunni Rashid Karame, the so-called *Nahj* ('method'), which was later called 'Democratic Front' (a term with favourable overtones in Western languages) —was of special importance in the 1960s. Karame had started the election campaign in 1962 with the unconstitutional demand that President Chehab should run a second time for the Presidency after his first six-year term of office had expired. However, Chehab finally refused to stand for a second term of office. Karame then assured his voters that he would nevertheless continue the *Nahj* of Chehab. With Egyptian support, he won the majority of seats in the new parliament for his bloc. As Prime Minister, Karame supported Nasser's 'Arab Socialism'—without, however, tackling social reforms in his own country and without founding his own political party. The country's three largest

23

political parties remained in opposition, at times uniting to
form a parliamentary bloc called *hilf* ('alliance').

Foreign observers who are unfamiliar with the peculiar
features of Lebanese parliamentary democracy frequently
confuse these voting blocs with parties. This is all the more
liable to happen because two long-established parties in
Lebanon, the *'Dastur* Bloc' and the 'National Bloc', use the
word 'bloc' as an integral part of their party name. Lawful
political parties already existed under French mandatory
rule, and had a greater influence on the country's development than the limited number of party-affiliated parliamen-
tarians in the various legislative periods indicates. During the
last two decades, the number of party members among the
M.P.s in the Beirut parliament has been constantly
increasing. This can be seen from the chart on page 25 (taken
from Jalal Zuwiyja, *The Parliamentary Election of Lebanon
1968*, Leiden, 1972).

Most of the political parties in Lebanon—those of the
democratic centre as well as the radical parties of the right
and left—were founded by Christians. Only one Sunni
Muslim and one Druze—respectively the Beirut Muslim
leader Adnan al Hakim and the Druze feudal lord Kamal
Jumblatt—have founded political parties during the whole of
modern Lebanese history.

No reliable statistics of the membership of different parties
are available for the last few years. For previous years too the
statistics are almost useless because of their low reliability.
One must also be careful in Lebanon with the epithets 'Right'
and 'Left', as these are taken from European parliamentary
parlance. The following survey does not exclude Right- and
Left-wing radical parties, but it begins with those parties
which, in both the last two decades, have operated officially
in Lebanon and were represented in parliament.

1. The Lebanese Kataeb Social Democratic Party (*al Kataeb
al lubnaniya, hizb ijtimai dimokrati*) is the full name of the
largest political party in Lebanon. The Arab word *kataeb,* is
a plural form and can be translated as 'battalions',
'regiments' or 'squadrons', also by the plural of the term
'phalanx' which is taken from the military vocabulary of
antiquity. Leftist opponents of Kataeb use the misleading
translation 'Falange', which is aimed at recalling the fascist

PARLIAMENTARY SEATS*

Parties	1951 No.	1951 %	1953 No.	1953 %	1957 No.	1957 %	1960 No.	1960 %	1964 No.	1964 %	1968 No.	1968 %
Dastur Party	†		†		†		5–8	6·60	5	5·05	3	3·03
Najjadah Party	†		†		†		1	1·01			1	1·01
Tashnaq Party (Armenians)	2	2·58	2	4·54	3	4·53	4	2·04	4	4·04	4	4·04
Progressive Socialist Party and its allies	3	3·87	2–4	6·80	3	4·53	6	6·06	6	6·06	6	6·06
National Liberal Party							4–5	4·50	6	6·06	9	9·09
National Bloc	2	2·58	3	6·71	4	6·04	6	6·06	2	2·02	6	6·06
Kataeb Party	3	3·87	1	2·27	1	1·51	6	6·06	4	4·04	9	9·09
Party-linked parliamentarians (*total*)	10		8–10		11		32–36		27		38	
Total of parliamentary seats	77		44		66		99		99		99	
Percentage of Party-linked parliamentarians		12·90		20·32		16·61		34·33		27·27		38·38

* Percentages are those of seats held by a party in relation to the total of parliamentary seats.
† No information available.

unity party of General Franco. However, this word does not accurately represent the party name in Arabic.

The founder and party leader of Kataeb is the Maronite Christian Pierre Gemayel, a chemist by profession, who was born in 1905 in the North Lebanese mountain town of Bikfaya. The Kataeb party was founded in 1936 as a youth organisation, and at first consisted overwhelmingly of students and friends of the Jesuit-run Université St. Joseph of Beirut. The party's major aim was to fight for Lebanese independence, and consequently it was repeatedly banned by the French mandatory authorities. As a political party, Kataeb still retained its former paramilitary organisation in 1943. During the 1950s its militia acquired the character of a Maronite home guard which tried to hold in check the armed units of the Arab Left in Lebanon, at first mainly the Nasserites but later the Palestinian guerrillas.

Kataeb stands for a democratic Lebanese state with laws guaranteeing equal opportunities to all citizens, irrespective of race, religious denomination or ideology. It was the first party represented in the Beirut parliament which opposed the confessionalism of Lebanese politics. In socio-political terms, it has always stood left of centre, and it has been responsible for introducing most of the social legislation in Lebanon during the last two decades.

The party is led by a politbureau. Before the civil war it controlled a strictly disciplined party apparatus in all the provinces of the country. During the war Kataeb took over important administrative duties in the regions defended by the Christian militia.

2. The 'National Bloc Party' (*hizb al kutlah al wataniyah*) was founded in 1934 by the Maronite leader Emile Eddé and is the oldest conservative party in Lebanon. In it Eddé brought together influential Christian citizens. He stood for a 'Small Lebanon', confined to the actual Lebanon mountain range. Under French mandatory rule, Eddé was President and head of state.

The programme of the 'National Bloc' is confined to a statement that its major task is to strengthen Lebanese sovereignty and work for the wellbeing of its citizens. The concrete definition of party ideology is entrusted to an *amid* ('chief') who is elected for a term of six years. After Emile

Eddé's death, his sons Raymond and Pierre took over the party leadership. In the 1960s, under the leadership of Raymond Eddé, the 'National Bloc' entered into an 'alliance' (*hilf*) of Christian parties together with the parties of the two other leading Maronite politicians, Gemayel and Chamoun. This electoral alliance was renounced by Eddé after the parliamentary elections were over. Supported by his 'National Bloc', Raymond Eddé tried three times (in 1958, 1970 and 1976) to capture the office of President, but failed on each occasion. As candidate of the radical Lebanese Left and of the Palestinian Arabs, he was defeated in 1976 by the Maronite banker Sarkis.

For several decades the 'National Bloc' could rely on solid support in the Northern port of Jubail and in the central plateau. In 1976, as a partisan of the Palestinian guerrillas, Raymond Eddé had to flee from his home-town Jubail, seeking refuge with the Palestinians in the West Beirut, and later went as an exile to Paris.

3. The 'National-Liberal Party' (*hizb al wataniyin al ahrar*). Its abbreviation is P.N.L. from the French party title '*Parti National Libéral*', and in Arabic people refer to it briefly as *Al Ahrar,* or 'the Liberals'. The party was founded in 1958 by Camille Chamoun. At that time the American government advised Chamoun to leave Lebanon when his term expired, together with his closest political friends, but this advice was not followed and instead he founded his new party, Al Ahrar. Within the next decade this party had become the second largest in Lebanon. To protect himself and his party supporters against those who had opposed him already in the turbulent year 1958, he formed a small home guard, called *Numur,* or 'Tigers'. This militia formed in 1967 the core of a larger organisation the structure of which was modelled on the Kataeb militia. Together with Kataeb, the Numur regarded as their duty the protection of the most important Christian residential areas against Palestinian guerrillas.

Chamoun is a descendant of the traditional Lebanese Maronite leadership, just as were the Eddés. But whereas the 'National Bloc' attracted exclusively Maronite voters, the National-Liberals also attracted a following among other Christian communities, and even among Lebanese Muslims. In the last decade, together with Kataeb, the National-

Liberals have fought for an improvement in social welfare legislation.

4. The Dastur Party (*hizb al ittihad al dasturi,* 'Party of the Constitutional Union'), founded in the 1930s by the Maronite Beshara al Khoury, has little influence today. It is a conservative Christian party consisting of friends of the first President of the independent Lebanese republic.

5. The Najjadeh Party ('Party of the Saviours') developed out of a Sunni Muslim youth organisation founded in 1936. For some time it was a kind of Muslim equivalent of the Kataeb of Pierre Gemayel. The Najjadeh fought, with the Kataeb, for Lebanese independence. For some time they were banned on account of their Pan-Arabist tendency, but in 1951 they were re-organised as a political party by the Beirut Muslim leader Adnan al Hakim. The motto of the Najjadeh party was 'Arab lands to the Arabs'. During the past decade the party, which stands for an 'Islamic civilisation', has lost its influence among the Sunni Muslims in Beirut to the parties of the Arab Left.

6. The 'Progressive Socialist Party' (*al hizb al taqaddumi al ishtiraki*) was founded in 1949 by the Druze Kemal Jumblatt, and until his death in 1977 it remained an important instrument of political power in the hands of this headstrong spokesman of the Lebanese Left. Jumblatt came from an influential Druze clan which originally lived in the Kurdish region of Anatolia. During the seventeenth century his family was accepted into the religious community of the Druzes, after an alliance between the warriors of Sheikh Ali Jumblatt and Emir Fakhreddin II. At the beginning of his political career, Kemal Jumblatt distributed some of his large landholdings among landless Druze peasants, but even at the time of his death he remained one of the richest feudal lords in Lebanon.

His Progressive Socialist Party fights in its programme against the influence of religious denominations in Lebanese politics. Nevertheless, his party members are predominantly Druze, and their families formerly constituted his feudal following. At the end of the civil war only a fraction of the Lebanese Druzes supported him. His opponent, the conser-

vative Druze Emir Majid Arslan, has worked ever since
Lebanon became politically independent for a relationship of
mutual trust between Druzes and Christians.

At the time when it was founded, the Progressive Socialist
Party, together with the political friends of Camille
Chamoun, opposed the government of Beshara al Khoury.
But when Khoury became President it broke with Chamoun.
During the crisis of 1958 Jumblatt's armed mountain
peasants were militant opponents of the government. In the
1960s Jumblatt's party adopted the pro-Soviet and pan-Arab
programme of President Nasser. After 1970 Jumblatt and his
party first supported the conservative President Franjiya.
During the civil war Jumblatt became the spokesman of the
Lebanese Left. He obtained this position as leader of both the
'Progressive Socialist Party' and the 'Front of National
Struggle' (*jibhat al nidal al watani*), which grouped itself
around his party. Later, this group adopted the name
'National Movement' (*al harakah al watanijah*).

7. The 'Syrian National Socialists'. This most important of
all Right-wing radical parties of the Arab Near East is
known in Lebanon even today by the initials P.P.S., which
conceal the French title '*Parti Populaire Syrien*', given to it in
the 1930s by the French mandatory authorities. Its official
title then was the 'Syrian National Socialist Party' (*al hizb al
suri al qaumi al ijtima'i*). In Lebanon this party has called
itself since 1958 simply the 'National Socialist Party' (*al hizb
al qaumi al ijtimai*).

The Syrian National Socialist Party was founded in 1934
by the Greek Orthodox Lebanese Antoun Saade. Its model
was the national socialism of Hitler with whose ideology
Saade, who was a teacher of German at the American
university in Beirut, had been well acquainted. The Syrian
National Socialists strive for a Syrian empire extending from
the Taurus mountains to the Red Sea and from Cyprus east
to the Gulf. In contrast to the later pan-Arab programme of
Nasser, in which Muhammad, the prophet of Islam, occupies
a place of honour both as '*Imam* [prayer leader] of Socialism'
and as an Arab leader, the Syrian National Socialists have
taken an anti-denominational and anti-religious stand ever
since their foundation. In Lebanon the party members are

drawn from all the religious communities represented in the country.

In 1949, after an unsuccessful military attempt to unite Lebanon with Syria, the founder of the party, Saade, was sentenced to death and executed in Beirut. However, the party's paramilitary organisation, which had already been built up in the 1930s, continued to play an important role in Lebanese politics after Saade's death. The Syrian National Socialists were fierce opponents of Nasser's policies and for this reason used their militia during the crisis of 1958 in support of President Chamoun. In 1962 they staged a *coup d'état* in Lebanon, but this was crushed. In the most recent years the party has split into rival factions, the strongest of which, under the leadership of the Lebanese Christian Inaam Raad, entered into an alliance with the Palestinian Left. Its strongholds today are the northern region of al Kurah, Tripoli and the Christian settlements Beit Meri and Brumana, east of Beirut. In some parts of the inner city of Beirut the National Socialists are also influential.

8. The Communist Party of Lebanon, already founded under French mandatory rule, is among the oldest Communist parties of the Near East. However, the Lebanese Communists have not been able to exert any real political influence since the country became independent. Because of its anti-constitutional objectives, it was declared illegal and thus the party has seldom made its presence felt publicly.

The smaller parties and organisations of the Lebanese Left have repeatedly changed their titles during the last decades. It therefore seems useful to enumerate them, in so far as they control their own militias, in Appendix I (page 71) which gives a survey of all the militia which fought in the Lebanese civil war.

VIII

THE PALESTINIAN REFUGEES AND THE ARAB STATES

Immediately after the end of the British mandate in Palestine, heavy fighting broke out between Jews and Arabs. More than half a million Arabs then left Palestine. Today it is still hotly debated to what degree this flood of refugees was the result of military action by the Jewish guerrillas or of misleading political propaganda by Arab states. After the end of the first Arab-Israeli war, several hundred thousand Palestinian Arabs came to live in Lebanon, Syria and the Gaza strip, which was administered by Egypt till 1967. All of these had fled from their old homes. Most were without means of support, and had to be cared for by their host-countries. To support them, a special agency of the United Nations, UNRWA (United Nations Relief and Works Agency), was founded. Annually since 1948, the United Nations General Assembly has requested Israel to allow the Palestinian refugees to return to their old homes or to recompense them for the losses they suffered during their flight. Israel has always refused to comply.

At first, the major burden of the support for the aid organisation UNRWA was borne by the three Western powers—the United States, Britain and France. Later, West Germany too began to send large donations to the refugee organisation. In contrast, all Communist states, with the exception of Yugoslavia, have refused to make any financial contribution to UNRWA.

UNRWA has improved living conditions in the refugee camps. It has organised a regular supply of staple foods to the people in the camps, and has established academic and trade schools for the children of the refugees. No Arab government, however, has ever agreed to integrate the refugees among the citizens of its own country. Through the continuing presence of the refugees, the Arabs hoped to force the Israelis to allow them to return to their old homes or recompense them for their losses.

Only in the 1960s did a change in the Arab attitude towards the refugees become noticeable. In 1964, at the first two Arab summit meetings called by Nasser, the Arab heads of state agreed, under Egyptian pressure, that a 'Palestine Liberation Organisation' should be constituted, which was to have political responsibility for the rights of the Palestine Arabs. During its first years, this organisation was mostly an instrument of the pro-Soviet power politics of Nasser. Its first General Secretary, the Palestinian Ahmad Shukairi, held the view that the most urgent task of the Palestine Arabs was the overthrow of the 'treacherous monarchies of Jordan and Saudi Arabia', to use the Egyptian expression of those times. Shukairi suggested that Palestine Arabs should prepare for a guerrilla war against Israel so that they could later 'throw the Jews into the sea'.

In the mid-1960s the Palestine Liberation Organisation began to train for guerrilla warfare young Palestine Arabs living in the refugee camps, and thus maintained by UNRWA. Protests by the United States that the camps maintained by a special agency of the United Nations were being used as centres for military training remained fruitless. The United States thereupon threatened to withdraw its contribution to UNRWA unless the refugee camps which that organisation supported ceased to be used as training centres for guerrillas. Shukairi answered that, if the United States should withdraw its contributions to UNRWA, Palestine Arabs would destroy all American property in Arab countries. At that time the United States did not wish to engage in an open struggle for power with the Palestine Arabs because the latter were supported by Egypt. Hence they ceased to protest against the military training of refugees, and continued to pay their contribution to UNWRA.

Already before the Arab–Israeli Six-Day War of June 1967, the popularity of Shukairi had declined, as he was not able to show any successes *vis-à-vis* Israel. Moreover, during the Six-Day War he adopted a passive attitude, and did not intervene in any way. This earned him the contempt of all Arabs. Immediately after the great defeat of the Arab states in that war, rival Palestinian organisations, competing with Shukairi's P.L.O., won many recruits. The most successful of these was *al-Fatah,* which had been founded in 1965 as a secret organisation.

The Fatah guerrillas were at first strongly opposed by Shukairi's followers and by Nasser's secret police. But after the Six-Day War, when al-Fatah began to fight a more active guerrilla war against Israel from East Jordan and South Lebanon, it soon began to win great prestige through the daring of its commandos, so that even the Egyptian Government started to negotiate with its leader, Yassir Arafat. In 1969, two years after the Six-Day War, Arafat was nominated as successor to the Palestinian Yahya Hammudeh, who had succeeded Shukairi as General Secretary of the P.L.O. In spite of this appointment, Arafat retained his office as spokesman of the al-Fatah guerrillas.

In contrast to Shukairi, who had called for the overthrow of the Jordanian and Saudi monarchies, the al-Fatah guerrilla organisation called on all Palestine Arabs, right from the start, to avoid struggles for power with Arab governments and to concentrate their efforts on the struggle with Israel. Arafat described skirmishes against individual Arab states—'battles on secondary battlefields'—as the greatest danger threatening the cause of the Palestinians. The leaders of al-Fatah promised that once they had won victory over the Zionist state of the Jews, they would establish a democratic state in Palestine. In this state Muslims, Christians and Jews would live on equal terms. Al-Fatah did not develop its own ideology, but confined itself to a pragmatic description of the goals of the guerrilla war. Thus the P.L.O. succeeded in maintaining good relations with socialist Arab states as well as with the conservative monarchies of the Arabian peninsula.

The *'Popular Front for the Liberation of Palestine'* was founded in 1967 by the Palestine Arab, Dr. George Habash, a paediatrician. As a rival to the Fatah organisation, the 'Popular Front' also began to train its men for guerrilla warfare. From the beginning it stood for Marxist principles. Its founder, Habash, was a Greek Orthodox Christian who, since before the Six-Day War, had been a leading member of the radical Left-wing 'Movement of Arab Nationalists' (*harakat al qaumiyin al Arab*). Most of the followers of this movement lived in Syria, Kuwait and Aden. Because of his subversive activities, Habash was arrested in Syria and remained in custody for several months. In contrast to the principles of al-Fatah, Habash followed the Shukairi line and demanded that the Palestinians should first of all start a popular war against the Arab monarchies and replace Lebanese democracy with a people's democracy based on the Marxist model. The 'Popular Front' of Habash was the first Palestinian guerrilla organisation to develop special tactics of hijacking aeroplanes and committing terrorist acts in Western Europe.

The *'Democratic Popular Front for the Liberation of Palestine'* split off from the Popular Front for the Liberation of Palestine, under the leadership of Nayef Hawatmeh from East Jordan, also a Christian. The 'Democratic Popular Front' differs from the 'Popular Front' of George Habash through its more clearly defined Marxist ideology. In contrast to Habash's organisation, the Democratic Popular Front at first held the view that it was not in the interests of the Palestine Arabs to commit acts of terrorism in Western Europe.

The Palestinian guerrilla organisation *al-Saiqa* ('Thunder') which was built up with the help of the Syrian Baath Party after the Six-Day War, collaborates closely with the Syrian government. Like the earlier Fatah guerrillas and like the Syrian President Assad in later years, the leader of Saiqa, the Palestine Arab Zuheir Muhsin, declared that the Palestinian guerrilla movement has only one task, namely of fighting Israel.

The brigades of the *'Palestine Liberation Army'*, stationed in Syria, Egypt, Jordan and Iraq, consist of Palestine Arabs who received a regular military training in the host-countries. Officers of the regular armed forces of these countries are serving in the various units of this 'Liberation Army'.

IX

THE PALESTINIAN ARABS
AND LEBANON

After the first Arab–Israeli war more than 100,000 refugees from Palestine came to Lebanon; according to some Lebanese estimates, the number was 170,000. Among these were 30,000 Maronite Christians who had only emigrated to Palestine during the First World War or later, and who, after their flight, found a home with their relatives. Other refugees, who had rescued part of their wealth from Palestine, found new homes in Lebanon, or emigrated with their assets to North or Latin America. In 1950 about 100,000—certainly not many more—unemployed Palestinian refugees had to be cared for by humanitarian aid organisations, but by 1975 the number of refugees in Lebanon who were cared for by UNRWA had almost doubled.

Some Palestinian refugees soon became influential in the Lebanese economy. In Beirut, the Middle East's banking centre, Intra Bank, which was headed by the Palestine Arab Yusuf Baidas, surpassed all the long-established local banking concerns in the scope of its transactions. In 1966, however, it went bankrupt through a too daring use of credit. Several Lebanese branches of Western firms, such as the oil company Aramco (Arabian American Oil Company), were headed by Palestinians. The refugee aid organisastion UNRWA also had its Middle Eastern headquarters in Beirut.

During the first two decades of their presence in Lebanon, the Palestine refugees did not emerge as a powerful factor politically. They were unarmed, and the Lebanese state policed the refugee camps. Moreover, the new Palestinian guerrilla organisations which arose after the Six-Day War were at first not unpopular with Lebanese Christians.

In December 1968, the Israelis reacted to the military operations of Palestinian guerrillas against their territory from South Lebanon with a surprise attack on Beirut airport, and Israeli airborne troops destroyed the greater part of

35

Lebanon's civil aviation fleet. This first retaliation on Lebanese territory gave a foretaste of the problems raised by the new guerrilla policy of the Palestinians, who were now operating from Lebanon without the consent or even the knowledge of the Lebanese army. Yet most of the victims of the first Israeli raids were Lebanese.

On 6 May 1969 President Charles Hélou declared in a television interview that Lebanon could only support the Palestine Arabs if they recognised the sovereignty and security of the Lebanese republic. On hearing this the Sunni Prime Minister Karame opposed his President and said that a system of co-ordination between the Palestinians and the Lebanese army could well reconcile a guerrilla war waged from Lebanese territory with the security interests of the Lebanese state. Yet even Karame could not prevent fresh fighting from continuing to erupt in May–October 1969 between the guerrillas and the Lebanese armed forces. Already at this time the refugee camps had been transformed into fortified positions for the guerrillas. Palestinian armed troops were entrenched in South Lebanon and near the Lebanese frontier with Syria. Without being able to protect Lebanon against Israeli retaliation, the guerrillas tried to force their host-country to adopt their own methods of making war on Israel.

In order to prevent further loss of life, the Lebanese General Bustani negotiated a secret treaty with the Palestinians, the so-called Cairo Agreement, signed on 3 November 1969. Its terms have for a long time been kept secret, but its general content soon became known. The Lebanese state declared itself ready to leave in the hands of the Palestinian guerrillas certain fortified positions in South Lebanon from which the latter could conduct the war against Israel; at the same time the state of Lebanon renounced its right to police the Palestinian refugee camps on its territory. In return the leaders of the P.L.O. and of the various guerrilla organisations united within it solemnly promised that in future they would discuss with the Lebanese army all their operations against Israel from Lebanese territory; all that would remain to the army therefore was a power of veto on all such guerrilla activities. The Palestinians also agreed not to store heavy weapons in the refugee camps and to forbid their cadres to carry arms outside the camps except in certain areas where the carrying of arms was specifically agreed upon by the Lebanese army.

This agreement was a political victory for the Palestinians. At the same time, by renouncing rights of sovereignty the Lebanese state had obtained no more than an important breathing-space. In Jordan too, tensions between the Government and the Palestinian guerrillas sharply increased in 1969. In 1970 the majority of guerrilla organisations agreed with the radical Left of the Palestine Arabs that their first task was to overthrow King Hussein. After that, the Jordanian capital Amman should become a 'Hanoi' in the war between the Palestinians and Israel. In the autumn of 1970, a civil war broke out in Jordan, in which the Palestinians were defeated by the Jordanian army. Tens of thousands of Palestinians, especially members of the radical guerrilla organisations, then sought refuge with their families in Lebanon. Most of them crossed the Lebanese border illegally by secret routes.

The Cairo Agreement between Lebanon and the Palestinians was broken by the Palestinians almost as soon as it was signed. The guerrillas intensified their operations against Israel from South Lebanon without obtaining the consent of the Lebanese army, and Israeli retaliatory raids destroyed many South Lebanese villages. On 10 April 1973 Israeli commandos landed in Beirut and Sidon, blew up Palestinian buildings and killed three Fatah leaders in their homes in Beirut.

This gave rise to a new test of strength between the Palestinian guerrillas and the Lebanese army, for the guerrillas accused the latter of excessive docility towards Israel. This fighting only ceased when the Lebanese government signed an additional agreement with the Palestinians at the Melkart Hotel in Beirut to supplement the Cairo Agreement of 1969. In the so-called Melkart Agreement, the signatories promised to adhere strictly to the Cairo Agreement. Representatives of the Lebanese army and of the Palestinian guerrilla organisations promised to form a joint commission to watch over the implementation of the two Lebanese–Palestinian agreements. This, however, was prevented by the Palestinians through the secession of important guerrilla organisations from the joint Palestinian high command. These guerrillas then fought against Israel from South Lebanon as independent units.

After the fourth Arab–Israeli War in October 1973, the Palestinian guerrillas in Lebanon allied themselves more closely with the Lebanese Left. In December 1973 they jointly demonstrated in Beirut against a visit of the American Secretary of State, Henry Kissinger. While Kissinger succeeded in 1974 in reducing step by step the tensions that existed between Egypt and Israel, the tensions between Palestinian Arabs and Lebanese Christians in Lebanon itself became ever more acute. Under the protection of the Cairo and Melkart Agreements, the Palestinians built up their refugee camps in Lebanon into genuine fortified positions. The small Lebanese army was too weak to prevent this. Guerrillas, uniformed and armed, moved freely through the streets of all Lebanese towns. The Soviet Union, Syria, Iraq and Libya provided the Palestinian guerrillas in Lebanon with all the arms they needed.

From 1973 onwards, in order to be prepared for the armed conflict that now appeared unavoidable, the militias and home guards of the Lebanese Christians began to train themselves and were trying to obtain weapons from other countries.

X

FROM THE OUTBREAK OF THE CIVIL WAR TO THE BEGINNING OF SARKIS' PRESIDENCY

The war in Lebanon began with heavy fighting between the Palestinian guerrillas and the Kataeb militia. This confrontation was provoked by the Palestinians. On 13 April 1975, a Sunday, the leader of the Kataeb Party, Gemayel, went to attend the consecration of a new church in the Christian suburb of Beirut, Ain Rummaneh. Armed Palestinian guerrillas approached the church in two cars, opened fire and shot four Christians dead, among them a well-known member of the Kataeb party. Within a few hours a bus carrying armed Palestinians drove through the same suburb; Christian militias stopped it and shot dead all the twenty-two men on board.

In judging this incident it is important to know that in times of political tension the religious communities in Lebanon have tried to protect their areas of settlement from incursions by armed outsiders. On 13 April the shooting which had taken place in the morning was already common knowledge throughout Beirut by the time the bus load of armed Palestinians arrived in Ain Rummaneh from the East Beirut refugee camp of Tell Zaatar. However, other important details have remained unclear. For example, it is not known to which Palestinian organisation the men who killed the four Christians in front of the church of Ain Rummaneh belonged. It is also not known whether all the Christian militiamen who shot the bus load of armed Palestinians belonged to the Kataeb party. It is certain, however, that the attack on the bus was provoked by a second invasion by Palestinians into a Christian area on a Christian public holiday.

The events of Ain Rummaneh soon set off further clashes in Beirut between the Palestinian guerrillas on the one side and the militia of the Kataeb party and the National Liberals on the other. From the fortified refugee camp of Tell Zaatar

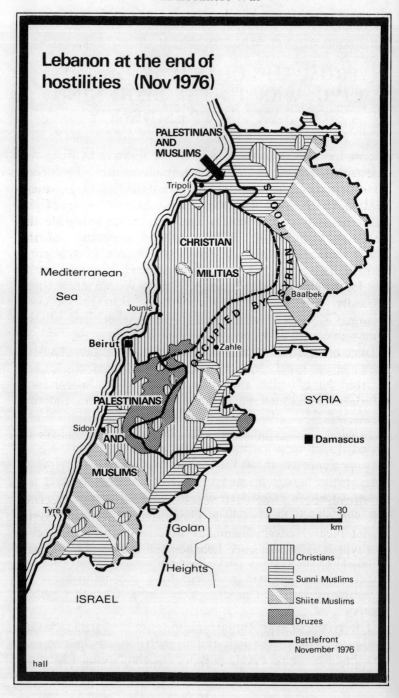

Lebanon at the end of hostilities (Nov 1976)

PALESTINIANS AND MUSLIMS

Tripoli

CHRISTIAN MILITIAS

Mediterranean Sea

Jounié

Baalbek

OCCUPIED BY SYRIAN TROOPS

Beirut

Zahle

PALESTINIANS

SYRIA

Sidon

AND

■ Damascus

MUSLIMS

Tyre

Golan

0   30
km

Heights

ISRAEL

Christians
Sunni Muslims
Shiite Muslims
Druzes
— Battlefront November 1976

hall

the Palestinians fired with mortars into the densely populated Christian quarter of Ashrafiya in East Beirut. Together with armed Shiite Muslims and with Communist militia fighters, the Palestinian guerrillas plundered the Christian quarters in the south-east of Beirut. After three days of heavy fighting the secretary-general of the Arab League, Mahmoud Riad, negotiated a ceasefire. But already next day intense fighting broke out again after unknown marksmen had shot at passers-by from rooftops in the centre of Beirut.

During the engagements of the subsequent weeks a number of tendencies became noticeable. First the fascist Lebanese 'National Socialists' and the radical Marxist wing of the Palestine guerrilla movement fought together alongside the Lebanese Communists, Nasserites and supporters of the Druze leader Jumblatt against the Lebanese Christian militias. The militias of the Left were at first supported by the followers of the influential Shiite *imam* Musa Sadr. Secondly, the militias of the Christian leaders (Kataeb, National Liberals, *Tanzim* militiamen, the home guard of the Zghorta uplands and smaller groups) united to achieve a joint defence of the most important Christian settlements. Thirdly, the Lebanese army remained neutral. And finally, the leaders of the P.L.O. and the al-Fatah guerrilla organisation refrained throughout this first phase of the war from allying themselves openly with the Palestinian and Lebanese Left-wing party. Only much later did it become known that from the outbreak of the fighting, al-Fatah had given active support to all organisations of the Lebanese Left fighting against the Christians.

Already during the first weeks of the war a very decisive role was played by the Soviet Union, Iraq, Libya and Syria. Soviet Near Eastern diplomacy welcomed unrest of a civil war type in Lebanon, since Lebanon had been considered part of the United States sphere of influence, and the fighting in Beirut diminished Western influence in the only Arab country which was ruled on the model of Western democracy. At the same time, the fighting neutralised the successes which the American Secretary of State, Kissinger, had achieved during his negotiations with Egypt and Israel. Already in 1975, the Kremlin was working in close collaboration with the governments of the oil-producing countries Iraq and Libya, which jointly provided the Lebanese and Palestinian Left with money and arms.

Syria, on the other hand, had tried to stabilise its influence by means of negotiations with the most important power groups in Lebanon. In order to secure a strong and lasting hold over the guerrilla organisations, Syria continued until as late as the summer of 1975 to deliver arms to the Fatah guerrillas. With Syrian support, the Lebanese Muslim Rashid Karame succeeded in June 1975 in forming an emergency government. The cabinet, which consisted of only six members, comprised representatives of the country's most important religious communities. For three months in the summer of 1975, the emergency government succeeded in maintaining a ceasefire, which was only interrupted by brief incidents.

Already during the first phase of the war, a new power factor was noticeable in Lebanon. This the Arabs called the 'Third Force'. The most important characteristic of this new force was that it re-started the shooting after each ceasefire agreement, and carried out planned murders so that the tensions between Christians and Muslims would be heightened. In this way the Third Force tried to transform the conflict of interests between the Palestine Arabs and the Lebanese into a religious war among the Lebanese themselves. Already in April and May 1975 several hundred young Lebanese Christians—mostly Maronites—had been kidnapped and murdered by unknown killers. These murders inspired acts of revenge by the Christian militias.

According to leading Lebanese politicians, these murders of Lebanese Christians were carried out by professional criminals in Beirut who were in the pay of Libya and Iraq. Besides these, guerrillas of the radical Palestinian Left, the Palestinian secret organisation 'Black September', and a group of Lebanese Nasserites whose militia began to call itself 'Murabitun' (meaning something like 'front-line fighters in a religious war'), were associated with the murder of Christians. After each ceasefire the Third Force succeeded through murderous attacks on especially vulnerable positions in reviving the fighting spirit of one belligerent or the other.

On 1 September 1975 Egypt and Israel signed an agreement under which Israel promised to withdraw its troops from the Suez Canal and from the Egyptian oilfields along the Gulf of Suez. Egypt and Israel also agreed to the joint supervision of all troop movements in the Sinai peninsula with American observers. A few days after the signing of this agreement, which was generally hailed as an important victory of American Near Eastern diplomacy, heavy fighting started once again in Lebanon. Jumblatt, as spokesman of the Lebanese Left, called for a general strike in the country on 15 September. This strike did not materialise, but instead heavy fighting erupted in the centre of Beirut between the Lebanese and Palestinian Left and the Christian militias. Also, the Palestinian Fatah guerrillas now fought openly on the side of the Lebanese Left. Evidently the new outbreak of fighting had been encouraged by Soviet diplomacy, which tried successfully to neutralise in Lebanon the advantage gained by Kissinger in Egypt. The Soviet Ambassador in Beirut, Soldatov, had previously been posted in Cuba and was considered a leading authority on urban guerrilla warfare.

In the new outbreak of fighting in September, armed troops of the Left began plundering the bazaars of the Christians in the city centre and the southern suburb of Haret Hureek. From the fortified refugee camps at Tell Zataar and Jisr al-Basha in East Beirut, Palestinian sabotage commandos blew up the most important industrial plants in the capital's eastern suburbs. In the East Beirut slum quarters of Karantina (Quarantaine) and Nabaa, the Palestinian guerrillas dug themselves in with heavy weapons and tried from there to cut off Beirut's most important Christian quarter, Ashrafiya, from the Christian North of the country. In order to defend the harbour of Beirut and the city centre against Palestinian attacks, Christian militias occupied the tall buildings of the city's hotel quarter. However, after heavy fighting against the united forces of the Palestinian guerrillas and the Lebanese Left, they had to abandon the hotel quarter and move further east.

On Saturday, 6 December, the bodies of four bodyguards of Beshir Gemayel were found in an eastern suburb of Beirut. Gemayel, son of the Kataeb leader Pierre Gemayel, had already achieved influence in Christian Lebanon as deputy commander of the Kataeb militia during the first year of the war. This killing on 'Black Saturday', which was on the eve of a visit by Pierre Gemayel to Damascus, caused a further intensification of the fighting.

During the following weeks the Christian militias encircled the guerrillas who had dug themselves into the Karantina slum quarter in East Beirut, and on 18 January 1976 succeeded in breaking their armed resistance. At the same time the militias of the Lebanese Left and Palestinian guerrillas besieged the Christian town of Damour south of Beirut. The inhabitants of Damour were evacuated in fishing boats to Jouniyeh. On 20 January 1976 the Palestinians and the militias of the Lebanese Left took Damour, and plundered and destroyed it.

In order to force a ceasefire, President Assad of Syria moved the units of the 'Palestine Liberation Army' stationed in Syria into the Bekaa valley in the east of the country. These Palestinian troops were accompanied by Syrian officers, and they brought about an end to the fighting in Beirut. The Lebanese President Franjiya then held negotiations with President Assad in Damascus, and on 14 February 1976 he announced a programme of internal political reforms. In future only 50 per cent of the seats in the Lebanese parliament would be allocated to Christians, not 55 per cent as hitherto. Moreover, the Prime Minister would no longer be nominated by the President, but elected by the majority in parliament. Religious affiliation would no longer be taken into account in the appointment of civil servants.

After the announcement of these reforms, many Lebanese believed that the war was over. The principal leaders of both the Lebanese Christians and the Muslims accepted the reforms. In Beirut the brigades of the 'Palestine Liberation Army' sent by Syria had formed a *cordon sanitaire* between the fronts. Economic life began to revive. But already a month later this new ceasefire had been destroyed. On 11 March the Lebanese General Aziz al Ahdab, together with the Lebanese troops stationed in West Beirut, united with the Palestinians and the Lebanese Left and tried to force President Franjiya to retire. Ahdab achieved nothing from his military *coup* except a split of the army into a wing loyal to President Franjiya and a wing which subsequently fought on the side of the Palestinians. In the Bekaa valley, mutinous Muslim troops rallied round the Lebanese Lieutenant Ahmad Khatib.

On 8 May, parliament met in Beirut in an emergency session to elect a successor to President Franjiya. His term of office did not expire till 22 September, yet there was speculation that the prospect of a change in the leadership of the country would make it easier for the Syrian government to negotiate a lasting ceasefire between the different parties. Only then should the new President take over from Franjiya. Elias Sarkis, governor of the Central Bank, was elected President with a large majority. The candidate of the Left and of the Palestinians, Raymond Eddé, received only a few votes. But not even after the election of a new President were Syria's efforts to achieve a ceasefire in Lebanon with the help of the Palestine Liberation Army successful.

Instead, the war spread to East Lebanon. Supported by Palestinian guerrillas and armed Muslim peasants, the troops of Lieutenant Ahmad Khatib began to besiege rural Christian towns and villages. Because the passes across the Lebanon Mountain range were blocked by snow, reinforcements from the Christian militias on the North Lebanese Mediterranean coast and along the western slope of the Lebanon Mountains could not reach these settlements. Hence the Christians in two large villages in the northern Bekaa valley and Christian leaders of the town of Zahle asked Syria for military protection.

On 1 June 1976 regular Syrian troops marched into Eastern Lebanon, raised the siege of the Christian villages, and crossed the Lebanon Mountains towards Beirut and Sidon. Thus the large Christian settlements of Eastern Lebanon were saved from Lieutenant Khatib's threatened attack. But the Syrian troops were met on their westward march by the united resistance of the Palestinian guerrilla organisations, the militias of the fascist Lebanese 'National Socialists' and the Lebanese Left. To avoid bloody street-fighting, the Syrian tanks halted on their march towards Beirut near the town of Sofar in the Lebanese mountains. However, the Syrian troops which had made for Sidon reached the most important airport in the country, south of Beirut.

The Palestine Liberation Organisation protested to the League of Arab States in Cairo at Syria's military intervention. Lebanon is a member of the League, as are the other nineteen Arab states. Nevertheless, without consulting a Lebanese representative, the Secretariat of the League called for a conference on Lebanon. It did this on a petition by the

Palestinians, sponsored by Egypt. This happened because
from March 1976 onwards the government of Egypt, which
had previously been neutral in the Lebanese war, began to
support the Palestinian guerrillas in Lebanon and the
Lebanese Left whom, from the early summer of 1976, Egypt
also provided with arms.

However, the Lebanese conference in Cairo did not
condemn Syria, as Egypt had hoped. Instead, the Arab states
decided to send to Beirut a peace force of the Arab League,
for which Syria, Libya, Saudi Arabia and the Sudan were
asked to provide troops. At first only Syria and Libya sent
soldiers to Beirut. During the summer months the Arab
League's peace force was occupied with its own problems,
because the Libyan detachment and the Egyptian representatives of the Arab League sought to neutralise each other's
activities.

However, as early as June the Egyptian secretary-general
of the Arab League confirmed that the League would
continue to recognise only Franjiya as President of Lebanon.
Among members of the League there was dissension on the
question as to who was Foreign Minister of Lebanon.
President Franjiya had appointed the Minister of the Interior,
Chamoun, as successor to the Greek Catholic Foreign
Minister Taqla, who had fled to Paris, and did not want to
return. According to the Lebanese constitution, the President
appoints and dismisses ministers without consulting the
Prime Minister. After the appointment of Chamoun,
however, the Prime Minister Karame declared that he was
deputy Foreign Minister acting for Taqla in his absence in
spite of the fact that Taqla had already been dismissed by the
President.

In July the Christian militias intensified their siege of the
fortified Palestinian camps of Tell Zaatar and Jisr al-Basha
east of Beirut, and after suffering heavy losses conquered
both camps. In return, Palestinian guerrillas from Tripoli
occupied the coastal town of Shikka. In a counter-offensive,
the Christians drove the Palestinians back to Tripoli and
occupied the rural town of Amioun, a stronghold of the
fascist Syrian National Socialists, who had allied themselves
with the Palestinians.

During the last weeks of Franjiya's term of office, Lebanon
was divided into three distinct political zones. North Lebanon

with East Beirut, as well as the greater part of the North Lebanese coast and the harbour of Jouniyeh, were controlled by the Christian militias. President Franjiya lived in this region in the rural town of Kfur, 8 kilometres north of Jouniyeh. The South of Lebanon, with West Beirut and the southern ports Sidon and Tyre, as well as Tripoli, were controlled by the Palestinian guerrillas and the militias of the Lebanese Left. The Bekaa valley in the east and the Akkar region in the north were controlled by Syrian troops.

On 23 September 1976 the new President, Elias Sarkis, succeeded President Franjiya. Sarkis took the oath of office at an extraordinary meeting of parliament in the eastern town of Chtaura, which had assembled under the protection of Syrian troops.

XI

SYRIAN PEACE TROOPS
IN BEIRUT

Already a short time before he took office, President Sarkis
had started negotiations with the Palestinians; he had been
urged to do this by Egyptian representatives of the Arab
League in Beirut. However, the discussions, which took place
at Chtaura, and which were also attended by the Syrians,
remained without positive results. At Chtaura, Sarkis suggested that as a sign of their goodwill, the Palestinians should
show their readiness to negotiate by withdrawing from the
Christian villages in the mountains immediately north of the
highway running from Beirut to Damascus. The Palestinian
leader Arafat declined to do so. At the beginning of October,
in a common offensive, Syrian troops and Christian militias
occupied this area which President Sarkis had requested
during the negotiations. In spite of heavy Palestinian
resistance, Syrian tanks penetrated as far as the holiday
resort of Bhamdun, which, as the crow flies, is no more than
20 kilometres from the centre of Beirut. The Palestinian
guerrillas, who fled from the villages north of the Damascus
highway, withdrew to the town of Aley, immediately west of
Bhamdun. Aley was also the headquarters of the Druze
leader Jumblatt.

There the fleeing Palestinian guerrillas came under heavy
fire from Syrian artillery. This was a highly dangerous
situation for the Palestinians, and the Saudi Arabian King
Khalid called the heads of state of Syria, Egypt and Kuwait,
as well as the new Lebanese President Sarkis and the
Palestinian leader Arafat, to peace talks at Riyadh. Syria
accepted the invitation and called off its heavy attack on
Aley. According to Lebanese experts on the military
situation, the conference at Riyadh prevented the strongest
units of the Palestinian guerrillas from suffering a crushing
defeat.

At the beginning of the Riyadh conference, President

Sadat of Egypt proposed a peace plan for Lebanon containing the following suggestions:

1. All military units in Lebanon should withdraw to the positions they had occupied at the beginning of the civil war on 13 April 1975;

2. Syrian troops should leave Lebanon;

3. A peace force manned by troops of several Arab countries should watch over the ceasefire in Lebanon;

4. The Cairo Agreement of 1969 should regulate again the relations between the Palestinians and the Lebanese Government.

The Arab heads of state and the Palestinian leader Arafat accepted the Egyptian proposal with one important modification: Syria should not withdraw its troops from Lebanon, but should integrate them into the proposed pan-Arab peace force.

The Riyadh conference (17–18 October 1976) was followed by one of Arab heads of state in Cairo (25–26 October). This summit conference confirmed in principle the peace plan of Riyadh and decided that the pan-Arab peace force for Lebanon should consist of 30,000 men. Of these, 20,000 should be Syrians, and further units should come from the Sudan, Saudi Arabia, North and South Yemen, and the United Arab Emirates. Several Arab countries agreed to bear the operational cost of the peace troops. The results of the two conferences were above all a success for the Syrian President Assad; for the most important Arab states had not only decided to tolerate a Syrian presence in Lebanon, but they had accorded to the Syrian troops in that country the status of a neutral peace force.

However, the new peace plan lacked clarity in some important respects, and therefore, right from the beginning, it contained the seeds of new conflicts. For example, it failed to define what was meant by the formula, originally recommended by Sadat, that the opposing forces in Lebanon should return to the positions they had held on 13 April 1975. Thus, should the soldiers of the Lebanese army, some of whom had fought on the side of the Christians and others on the side of the Palestinians, live together again in the same military barracks? The Lebanese regarded such an idea as utopian, for there were insurmountable divisions within the ranks of the country's army. And to which territory should those

Christian militias withdraw which had only been formed during the civil war? If they should disband, the Palestinian guerrillas would be the most powerful military force in Lebanon.

The reference to the Cairo Agreement was unfortunate too. This secret agreement of 1969 between the government of Lebanon and the Palestine Liberation Organisation had been reached only through pressure from Egypt. It had already proved impracticable, even before the civil war, as a means of overcoming the differences between the Lebanese government and the Palestinian guerrillas. The limited freedom of action *vis-à-vis* Israel, which the Cairo agreement had granted to the guerrillas in Lebanon, exposed the weak and unprotected Lebanese state again and again to retaliatory raids from Israel. The Lebanese state, seriously weakened through the civil war, will be quite incapable of bearing the burden of a guerrilla army operating from its southern territory.

Immediately after the Cairo conference of the Arab heads of state on Lebanon, new clashes between a Christian militia, the 'Army for the Liberation of Occupied South Lebanon' and Palestinian guerrillas were reported from the region immediately north of the Lebanese-Israeli border. The Christian militia was supported from across the border with Israel by Israeli artillery in its fight against he Palestinians. For the Lebanese Christians as well as for the Israelis, it was essential after the Lebanon conference in October to prevent Palestinian guerrilla troops from entrenching themselves along the Israeli border by invoking the Cairo Agreement of 1969.

At the beginning of November the Syrian troops, now called peace troops, occupied the town of Aley. President Sarkis entrusted the Lebanese Muslim, Brigadier-General Ahmad al Hajj, with the supreme command of the Syrian peace troops and the peace troops from Saudi Arabia, Sudan and Libya which had been stationed in Lebanon since the summer of 1976. The contingents of peace troops from the United Arab Emirates, which had been announced at the Cairo conference, only arrived many weeks later. Supported merely by small Sudanese and Libyan units, the Syrian troops advanced step by step on Beirut and on 15 November they occupied the heart of the city. The Syrians also took over control of Beirut airport, the South Lebanese port of Sidon, the northern port of Tripoli and the most important highways in the country.

In the centre of Beirut, the barricades erected by the opposing forces in the civil war were taken down. By the end of November Syrian soldiers were in occupation of the most important places and public buildings in both sections of the city, which had been divided during the civil war. Only in South Lebanon were Palestinian guerrillas still fighting against Christian militias. The important Palestinian guerrilla organisations had evacuated their front-line positions in the capital and withdrawn to South Lebanon and to the refugee camps south of Beirut. President Sarkis began negotiating the formation of a new cabinet with the leaders of Lebanese Christians and Muslims.

However, the suspicion between the two important population groups continued. The Christians were hesitant to visit West Beirut or the Muslim territory in the north of the country. The Muslims avoided visiting territory previously defended by Christian militias. The Palestinian guerrilla organisations refused to give up control of their heavy arms to the peace troops.

In spite of this, some optimists in Beirut thought at the end of 1976 that the forced ceasefire achieved by Syrian troops had initiated peace. They thought that President Sarkis would now proceed, slowly but consistently, to reconcile the embattled Christians and Muslims and would create a unified state structure for the whole country. According to this optimistic vision of the future, Palestinian refugees and guerrilla organisations could find a home in West Jordan and in Gaza. These territories, occupied since June 1967 by Israeli troops, should become the new state of 'Palestine' and be administered by a government formed of Palestinian Arabs, but grouped with either Israel or Jordan into a federal state. A precondition for this plan was a quick success for the Near East conference at Geneva, which some observers in Beirut hoped would reconvene in Spring 1977.

Sceptical observers believed, however, that even after the occupation of the city centre of Beirut by Syrian troops, a long-drawn-out crisis could be expected. The pessimists in Beirut argued that the Palestinian guerrilla organisations had obtained a much-desired breathing-space as the result of the ceasefire. Indeed, there were indications by the beginning of December that the guerrillas in Lebanon were preparing themselves for a long drawn out conflict by working out new methods, in particular the formation of secret Marxist cells. Experts in the tactics of the guerrilla organisations feared that the Palestinians were only waiting for a suitable time when the Lebanese—Muslims as well as Christians—would begin to see the presence of the Syrian peace troops in their country as a burden. At that point the Palestinians would start a new guerrilla war against the widely-scattered Syrian troops. They expected that the economic losses caused by the war would also win support for the Palestinians from the radical Lebanese Left among the Christians in Northern Lebanon.

In such an atmosphere of mistrust and sceptical specu-lation about the future, President Sarkis formed his first government on 9 December. The banker Salim al Hoss, a politically colourless Sunni Muslim, offered his services as prime minister; he was reckoned to be one of the closer friends of President Sarkis. The traditional distribution of ministerial office according to religious affiliation was con-tinued in the eight-member cabinet of Hoss. The Christians received four portfolios, the Muslims three and the Druzes one. All the members of the new government had kept aloof from politics during the civil war; several had spent the worst months of the war outside the country. The new ministers were recommended to the Lebanese public as techno-crats—non-political experts having no links with the parties represented in Parliament.

On 23 December Parliament empowered the government to rule by emergency decree for the next six months. The responsibility of members of parliament for the state during this time was restricted to an advisory role in parliamentary committees. The most important instrument of power at the disposal of President Sarkis was the Arab peace force, composed mainly of Syrian troops. Syria's influence on the peace force was considerable, although formally the force was commanded by a Lebanese officer who was responsible only to the Lebanese head of state. The first force commander to be appointed by President Sarkis was Colonel Ahmad al Hajj.

XII

THE POLITICS OF BALANCE VERSUS TERROR

On 3 January 1977 a big explosion shook the Christian district of Ashrafiya in Beirut. Forty Lebanese Christians were killed outright, and a further twenty died later from their injuries in hospitals (see plate 8). The alliance of the Palestinian guerrillas and the Lebanese Left was regarded as being responsible for this bomb attack, which triggered off acts of revenge against the Palestinians by militant Christians. Nevertheless, President Sarkis made notable progress in the following weeks with his policy of pacification and reduction of tension. Beirut remained a city divided politically by the civil war frontiers, but the number of Lebanese Christians who went to work daily in West Beirut gradually increased, and Lebanese Christians also began, hesitantly, to revisit the Christian parts of the city.

At first the Sarkis government showed no sign of having a political programme. Only gradually did it become clear that President Sarkis was striving towards a reconciliation between the major Christian parties of the country on one side and—on the other side—the Right and Left radical groups allied with the Palestinian guerrillas, by a depoliticisation of public life. An official press censorship ordered by the government was to serve the same purpose. In the early months of 1977 the new government was engaged in intensive planning of economic reconstruction. But Prime Minister Hoss avoided any discussion of the political future, which Christian leaders were demanding.

The two largest parties in Lebanon, the Kataeb Party and the National-Liberal Party, demanded reorganisation of political life on the basis of a federal constitution: the national territory should be divided into several predominantly Christian and predominantly Muslim cantons, which should receive extensive administrative autonomy. The army of the federal state should consist of separately recruited Christian and Muslim units. The Christian leaders

53

declared that trust between Christians, Muslims and Druzes could only be re-established through discussion and negotiation between religious communities and parties concerning the reorganisation of public life.

President Sarkis was not of this opinion, and the traditional leaders of the Lebanese Muslims also did not want negotiations concerning a new constitution. During the civil war they had had to yield their influence to the fighting units of the Palestinian guerrillas, and even after the occupation of the inner city of Beirut by the Syrian peace force, the Palestinians remained the strongest political force in the areas which they had controlled in the war. Before the war and during its early stages, the Lebanese Muslims had demanded political reform with great vigour.

Their refusal in 1977 to negotiate with the Christian leaders, who also advocated internal reforms, had several quite distinct motives. First, the leaders of the Sunni Muslims in Lebanon feared that during negotiations with the Christian leaders, their weakness within their own community as well as in their relations with the Palestinians would become too clearly apparent. Secondly, the *ulema* ('learned men') of the Sunni Muslims did not wish even to consider the demand of the Lebanese Left and the Palestinian leaders for the secularisation of the Lebanese state. The Kataeb Party and their allies within the 'Lebanese Front' had agreed on the replacement of family law that was governed by religious confession by one which should be binding upon all religious denominations equally. This would have meant the introduction of uniform legislation inspired by modern Western legal norms in the field of marriage law as well. This was decisively rejected by the spiritual leaders of the Lebanese Muslims who objected most of all to marriages being permitted between Muslim women and Christian men. According to Islamic law, the only marriages between Muslim women and Christian men that are legal are those in which the Christian has first been converted to Islam. This refusal by Muslim religious leaders to countenance the secularisation of Lebanese laws blocked the suggestions for reform made by the Christian parties and the Lebanese Left alike.

Thirdly, the Lebanese Muslims and Druzes had no interest in negotiations with the Christians because of their fear that

PLATES

1 Christian militiamen on the road cleared through snow several metres deep in the summer of 1976 to reach the East Lebanese village of Deir al-Ahmar, which was besieged by several thousand armed Lebanese Muslims and Palestinian guerrillas.

2. At the beginning of July 1976, Palestinian guerrillas occupied the North Lebanese coastal settlement of Shikka for two days and murdered all the Christians they could find. Shown here is a mass grave for the victims of the Shikka massacre, in front of a destroyed Maronite burial chamber.

3. A private dwelling in Shikka, as the Christian militia found it when they recaptured the settlement.

4. The Church of Our Lady of Mekallis after its desecration by Palestinian troops from Tell Zaatar refugee camp.

5. The industrial district of Mekallis close to Tell Zaatar, destroyed by the Palestinians.

6. A tank of the 'Arab Army of Lebanon', which fought on the side of the Palestinians in the civil war, after its capture on the central Lebanese high plateau by Syrian troops. The inscription reads 'The hero Ahmad al Khatib, hope of the Lebanese masses'. This man was a deserter to the Palestinians (see pages 44–5).

7. Graffiti on a wall: the party emblem of the fascist 'National Socialists', allies of the Palestinian guerrillas in Lebanon – a rounded swastika – seen alongside the hammer and sickle of the Communists. (Metain, Upper Lebanon.)

8. Destruction caused by a Palestinian terrorist bomb explosion in the Christian eastern sector of Beirut, January 1977, in which sixty lives were lost. Because of censorship, no photographs were published in the West.

(*Photographs:* 1, 2, 4, 6, 7, *Frankfurter Allgemeine Zeitung;* 3, 5, 8, the Lebanese Forces)

1

حرف
علامة
سنة ١٧٦

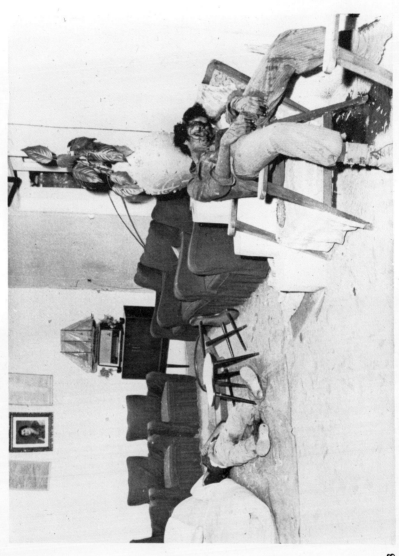

3

4

6

7

8

in that direction lay a federal constitution. The Muslims were also suspicious that their own position would be weakened and the unity of the Christians strengthened if there were to be recognition, through the holding of official negotiations between Christians and Muslims, that fundamental differences between the two cultures existed.

In this discussion President Sarkis supported the Muslim position. Sarkis held the view that the re-establishment of national unity should be initiated not by negotiations but through the politics of 'balance'. He refused a decentralisation of administration which might have encouraged a federal constitution. The army too should be reconstructed as a mixed force, comprising Christians, Muslims and Druzes. In this the President followed the example of his one-time master and political mentor President Chehab (1958–64), whose adviser and head of chancery he had been. Through a shrewd balancing act and a gradual compromise between conflicting opinions, President Chehab had re-established the national unity of the country after the crisis of 1958, at the cost however of inner stability and with major concessions to the Lebanese Left and its protector, the 'United Arab Republic' of President Nasser.

The policy of balance pursued by Sarkis in 1977 meant that he never publicly charged the Palestinians with responsibility for the outbreak of the civil war or for the crimes committed by the Palestinian guerrillas during the war. Also, the national broadcasting service in Beirut returned to the euphemism customary in some Arab countries and, in mentioning the guerrillas, alluded only to the Palestinian 'resistance movement' or even the 'Palestinian brothers' whose rights in Palestine all Arab states were obliged to support. The government of Hoss remained silent about the sufferings of the Lebanese during the civil war as if there had always been uninterrupted peace. The Christian parties criticised this ostrich-like attitude of the Sarkis administration: the Hoss cabinet was building on sand if it tried to improve the national economy without getting to grips with the political causes of the civil war. This was the reproach made against the new prime minister by Camille Chamoun, the leader of the 'Lebanese Front'.

With the aid of the Arab peace force, Sarkis was able to pacify to some extent the areas in which fighting had taken place. After the agreement of Riyadh, both the belligerent parties were required first of all to surrender their heavy weapons to the peace force. The Christian militia did so, surrendering their tanks and heavy artillery. However, the Palestinian guerrillas refused to part with their heavy weapons. Some of the Palestinian armed units moved away with their heavy weapons from West Beirut to the south of the country; also the fortified Palestinian encampments around Beirut airport kept their weapons. President Sarkis—as commander-in-chief of the peace troops—did not agree to disarm the camps by force. The Palestinians were not slow to observe that nobody was prepared to compel them to fulfil their side of the armistice agreement. Arafat, the secretary-general of the Palestine Liberation Organisation, had signed the Riyadh Agreement as representative of the Palestinian guerrillas, along with the heads of state of Lebanon, Syria, Egypt, Saudi Arabia and Kuwait. But already in May 1977 he publicly dissociated himself from the responsibilities he had undertaken in Riyadh. On 23 May 1977, at Abu Dhabi, when asked by journalists to comment on the demand of the Arab peace force and the Lebanese Christians that the camps in Lebanon be disarmed, he declared: 'As long as we live, we will not give up our weapons to anyone.'

XIII

A NEW MASSACRE OF CHRISTIANS AND THE GRADUAL CRUMBLING OF THE ARMISTICE

On 16 March 1977, unidentified assailants murdered the Druze chief Kemal Jumblatt near Baaklin, in the Shouf mountain district which is in the centre of the Lebanon mountains and densely populated by Druzes. Jumblatt, who during the war was the leader of the united Lebanese Left which called itself the 'National Movement', had despite this never ceased to be the most influential tribal chief and feudal lord among the Lebanese Druzes. At first no solution could be found to the murder. Well-informed observers in the country agreed unanimously that the Lebanese Christians were not responsible; yet the Christians in the Shouf highlands became the victims of bloody acts of revenge by Druzes. According to eye-witness accounts by survivors in the villages of Mazraat al-Shouf, Baruk, Maaser al-Shouf, Betnat and Kafar Nabrekh, which were inhabited by both Christians and Druzes, dozens of Christians were murdered and their houses looted by their Druze fellow-villagers in the hours following the murder. Reliable estimates put the total of Christian victims in the massacre that followed Jumblatt's murder at 130. Men, women, children and the old were killed indiscriminately with axes, iron bars or by knifing. Some Druze families protected Christian friends who sought shelter in their houses, but these were the exceptions. Several thousand Christians fled after the massacre from the Shouf highlands to the Christian settlement areas in the north of the country. Because of the press censorship imposed by the Hoss government in Beirut, only incomplete reports of these tragic events reached the outside world.

After Jumblatt's murder and the massacre of Christians that followed it, the gulf of mistrust between Christians on one side and, on the other side, Muslims and their Druze allies became even wider than before. In Beirut, the Arab peace force succeeded in preventing a renewed outbreak of fighting, but in the south fighting intensified from time to time: the Arab peace force could not exercise effective control over the Christian villages immediately north of the border between Lebanon and Israel, and over the Palestinian guerrilla units stationed in this area of the country. The Israeli government had already declared in 1976 that any forward movement of Syrian troops—which formed the bulk of the Arab peace force—in the vicinity of the frontier would be regarded as a threat; Israel reserved to itself the right of pre-emptive attack if non-Lebanese troops should move across the 'red line', the northern limit of an area which Israel declared a safety zone. Where exactly the 'red line' ran, Israel did not make public, but it was supposed to follow the course of the Litani river in South Lebanon.

The Christian villages in the frontier zone had armed themselves in 1976 as protection against the Palestinian guerrillas. Israel supported these villages: wounded Lebanese Christians from the south of the country were treated in Israeli hospitals, and Israel provided food and medical supplies for the villages. It was said that the Christian militia in the villages received ammunition from Israel as well. Pressure on the villages increased in the last weeks of 1976 when guerrilla combat units moved, with their arms, from their strong points in the inner city of Beirut into the south of Lebanon. The Palestinians received military supplies from their traditional allies, Libya, Iraq and the Soviet Union, through the southern port of Tyre.

The Riyadh Agreement of October 1976 had laid down the conditions for the entry of Arab peace troops into Beirut. A commission formed by representatives of the four guarantor-nations—Syria, Egypt, Saudi Arabia and Kuwait—were to supervise the carrying-out of the agreement. The Commission of Four met several times after the peace force had occupied the inner city of Beirut. During those meetings, most of its members sided with the Palestinians. When, in accordance with the agreement, the Christian militia had surrendered its heavy weapons to the Arab peace force, the Kuwaiti ambassador in Beirut, who represented his country on the Commission of Four, argued that the Palestinian guerrillas needed to retain their weapons in order to be prepared for a war with Israel. The ambassador hinted at the same time that Kuwait would give Lebanon aid for reconstruction only when the Lebanese became more accomodating to the Palestinian guerrillas. In Kuwait, radical groups of Palestinians—especially the Marxist 'Popular Front for the Liberation of Palestine' led by the Christian George Habash—had at their disposal considerable political influence. The ruling family feared that to take up a position against the interest of the Palestinian guerrillas in Lebanon might cause unrest, or even a Palestinian *coup d'état*, in Kuwait. Thus a breach by the Palestinians of the Riyadh armistice agreement was not merely tolerated by Kuwait but also shielded from public criticism.

At the climax of the fighting in the civil war, Egypt had supported the Palestinian guerrillas and Kemal Jumblatt, the leader of the Lebanese Left. Because of its dependence on economic aid from Saudi Arabia and Kuwait, Egypt was not prepared to take its own initiative in the Commission of Four. Like Kuwait, Saudi Arabia was inclined, owing to similar internal political considerations, to give tacit approval to the continuing violations by the Palestinians of the Riyadh armistice agreement.

On the other hand, there were increasing clashes in the western sector of Beirut between Palestinian guerrillas of the Saiqa organisation which followed the political line of the Syrian Government and other Palestinian organisations associated with the governments of Iraq and Libya. According to sources close to the Sarkis administration, the organisations against which the Saiqa guerrillas were fighting were consistent supporters of the so-called 'Refusal Front', i.e. guerrilla units which were hostile to any peace contacts of Arab governments with Israel. Politically, the most important guerrilla unit within the 'Refusal Front' was the 'People's Front for the Liberation of Palestine' led by Habash. Another powerful opponent of the Saiqa partisans was al-Fatah, the strongest Palestinian guerrilla organisation, although it was not counted as belonging to the 'Refusal Front'.

The former refugee camps of the Palestinians in West Beirut, fortified for many years past, formed a semi-circle around the international airport of Beirut and controlled the roads between it and the inner city. These camps were often surrounded by the Syrian units of the peace troops, but the differences between the Syrians and the guerrillas who refused to give up their weapons were mainly settled by negotiation. At the end of June 1977 heavy fighting broke out between the Saiqa units and the guerrilla organisations of the 'Refusal Front'. It was said that this fighting was sparked off when 'Refusal Front' guerrillas blew up an office of the Saiqa guerrillas. When the Arab peace force had re-established the ceasefire, Arafat, the secretary-general of the P.L.O., called together the leaders of all the Palestinian fighting organisations for consultations in Beirut.

In spite of their internal differences, the Palestinian politicians pursued basically the same tactics: they did not openly oppose the Arab peace force, yet they retained their heavy weapons in their fortified camps, and refused to fulfil the conditions of the Riyadh armistice agreement. As a success President Sarkis could point to a certain normalisation of everyday life in the country's capital city. However, Beirut remained politically divided into two sectors. Also, the rest of Lebanon continued to be divided into zones respectively under Christian or Syrian influence, or actually controlled by the Palestinians.

In the spring of 1977, when Kuwait sided more and more openly with the Palestinians, the question was discussed in the 'Lebanese Front' (the political union of Lebanese Christians) whether the Cairo treaty signed in 1969, together with its supplementary agreement, could still form the basis of relations between the government of Lebanon and the Palestinian guerrilla units on Lebanese territory. In June 1977 the leaders of the 'Lebanese Front' were considering the idea of declaring the Cairo treaty of 1969 null and void in view of the continual violations of the treaty by guerrilla units following the Riyadh armistice agreement. However, after energetic intervention by the Syrian government, the Christian leaders abstained from publicly revoking the treaty.

XIV

THE LEBANESE WAR:
REALITY AND PROPAGANDA

By tradition, the Papal Nuncio is the doyen of the diplomatic corps in Lebanon. In March 1977, when questioned by foreign journalists as to the way in which foreign states had communicated with the Lebanese head of state, the Nuncio, Bruniera, said that during the civil war the diplomatic corps had fled. In the end it was he, as doyen, who was representing the entire diplomatic corps to the Lebanese President.

This remarkable statement of the Papal Nuncio offered the key to many strange reactions among Western countries during the final months before the entry of the Arab peace force into Beirut. The presidential palace at Baabda near Beirut is in an area which was always controlled by Christian militia during the fighting, but it is situated in the immediate vicinity of the civil war front. After the failure of the *coup* by the Lebanese General Ahdab on 11 March 1976, the palace at Baabda was fired upon by the Palestinian guerrillas and their Lebanese allies. President Franjiya then moved the presidential seat, until the end of his term of office, to Kfur in the mountains near the Christian port of Jouniyeh, north of Beirut.

The embassies of the United States and the Soviet Union, as well as those of the nine member-states of the European Economic Community, are situated in West Beirut. On 17 June 1976, Mr. Meloy, the United States ambassador, was assassinated with two companions as he was attempting to drive from West Beirut to the Christian sector of East Beirut. Evidently Palestinian guerrillas were responsible. This murder had decisive consequences for relations between Western diplomatic missions and the Lebanese head of state. Even after weeks had passed following the murder, no Western head of mission dared to visit President Franjiya in Kfur. Only the Nuncio remained in constant touch with the Lebanese head of state.

In the summer of 1976 the diplomatic missions of the nine

countries of the E.E.C. bowed to pressure from the
Palestinian guerrillas and interrupted relations with the
Lebanese Foreign Minister. In July of the previous year, the
Greek Catholic Philippe Taqla had been appointed Foreign
Minister, but when the fighting in Beirut intensified he left
the country and stayed abroad for many months. As his
successor President Franjiya appointed Camille Chamoun,
the leader of the National Liberal Party, on 16 June 1976.
Under the Lebanese constitution, the President is empowered
to appoint and dismiss ministers without obtaining the
consent of the Prime Minister. The Prime Minister at that
time, the Sunni Muslim Karame, protested against Chamoun's
appointment to the Foreign Ministry and declared that he
himself was still acting Foreign Minister of Lebanon, as he
had been before when Takla was absent from Beirut. Karame
did not leave the West sector of Beirut, which was controlled
by the Palestinians, and it was there and with him that the
diplomatic representatives of the E.E.C. states communicated. They boycotted Chamoun out of fear of the Palestinian
murder commandos. In despatches to their governments, the
European diplomats took the untenable view that it was open
to dispute who was Foreign Minister of Lebanon—Chamoun
or Karame—and thus impossible for them to decide on the
matter.

Thus in the summer of 1976 there was a strange symbiosis
in Beirut between Western diplomats on the one hand and
Palestinian guerrillas and the militia of the Lebanese Muslims on the other. The West German embassy moved into a
new office at this time, the actual removal being guarded by
the 'Murabitun' militia led by the professional killer Koleilat,
who had been responsible for the murder of the Lebanese
publisher Mruwweh in 1965. In the late summer of 1976 the
United States government evacuated American citizens from
West Beirut using landing-craft of the Sixth Fleet: the
surrounding coastal area was guarded by Palestinian Fatah
guerrillas with tanks and infantry weapons to safeguard the
embarkation.

Like the embassies, the Western news agencies and most
correspondents of Western newspapers and broadcasting
networks had their offices in the Palestinian-controlled
western area of Beirut. The central post office is also situated
there, so it was therefore only from West Beirut that these

correspondents could cable, telephone or teleprint their reports. For months, cable and telex contact between the Christian eastern part of the city and the outside word was cut off. Just as the Palestinians had terrorised the diplomats by the murder of the American ambassador, so they intimidated the Western press correspondents in West Beirut by the murder of the Lebanese permanent correspondent of the Paris daily newspaper *Le Monde*, Edouard Saab. In his reports, Saab had presented the viewpoint of the Palestinian guerrillas and the Lebanese Left favourably; yet the Palestinian terrorists murdered him. They kidnapped in West Beirut the Belgian press photographer Marc Thirion who knew Lebanon well and had taken pictures of Palestinian guerrillas and Christian militias in action during the early stages of the war. No traces of Thirion were ever found. After these events, all Western correspondents felt themselves threatened by the Palestinians. They therefore began, in their own news reports on the civil war, to take up more and more the language of the Palestinian guerrillas in order, as they thought, to gain the Palestinians' favour and so protect themselves. Thus Palestinian horror propaganda against the Lebanese Christians found its way into reports by Western journalists.

During the civil war the Palestinian guerrillas put forward a clearly defined concept of psychological warfare. Their propaganda principles can be summarised as follows:

1. In Lebanon, Left or 'progressive' Muslims fight against Right or 'reactionary', or even 'fascist' Christians.
2. In the traditional distribution of power in Lebanon, the Muslims were at a disadvantage, since the Christians—especially the Maronites—ensured for themselves too large a share in parliamentary representation and in the government.
3. In Lebanon the Christians are rich, the Muslims are poor, and the Palestinians live in miserable camps at a bare subsistence level.
4. The Lebanese Christians are 'isolationist' and 'separatist'. In order to preserve their privileges they strive for a division of the country.
5. The Lebanese Christians are modern Crusaders. They fight under the sign of the Cross and thus prevent a reconciliation between Christendom and Islam.

6. The Lebanese Christians committed grave crimes in the civil war. The Lebanese Left and their allies, on the other hand, fought a just revolutionary people's war.

7. The civil war was an 'imperialist, Zionist and reactionary plot'. The 'imperialist United States' worked closely with the Zionist Jewish state of Israel, and with Syria as an agent of imperialism, in order to assist the reactionary Lebanese Christians to obtain victory.

To obtain an objective view of the events it is essential that one appreciates the true nature of this way of thinking and the slogans associated with it. They do not present facts, but are a deliberate distortion of the truth by one of the parties to the civil war—in other words, political propaganda. For a long time the Christians had no overriding concept of an information policy of their own to counteract the propaganda of the Palestinian guerrillas and the Lebanese Left. They knew only the rules of parliamentary democracy, and were almost defenceless against the aggressive horror propaganda of their opponents.

The principles of the Palestinian guerrillas quoted above were given such extensive currency in the West that it seems appropriate at this point to rectify them by means of a counter-exposition:

1. In the civil war, 'Right-wing' Christians did not fight 'Left-wing' Muslims. The parties united in the 'Lebanese Front' and their militia defended themselves against the unprovoked attacks of the Palestinian guerrillas and their Lebanese allies. The two most important parties within the 'Lebanese Front', namely the socialist Kataeb Party and the National-Liberal Party, are not on the Right of the Lebanese party spectrum, but represent the parliamentary centre.

There is only one large radical party of the Right—the fascist National Socialists (P.P.S.). The militia of this party fought on the side of the Palestinians in the civil war. The slogan 'Right-wing Christians' corresponds as little to political reality in Lebanon as does the concept of 'progressive Muslims'. Among the main opponents of the 'Lebanese Front'—who were not Muslims as such but Palestinian guerrillas—many Christians were to be found. In so far as the Lebanese Muslims engage in politics, they are more a consistently conservative force. The *Imam* of the Shiite Muslims, Musa Sadr, can by no stretch of the imagination be classified as a 'Left-wing Muslim'. In the war, the *Imam* at first supported the Palestinians and the Lebanese Marxist Left, but then drew closer to the Syrians, and in the last year of the war steered an unsteady course between several parties.

2. It has already been pointed out that reliable statistics of recent date concerning the percentages of the whole Lebanese population and of the various religious denominations are not available. The French Jesuit, Michel Riquet, in his pamphlet *Les Maronites au Liban* (Geneva 1977), quoted Lebanese statistics according to which 52.7 per cent of the population were Christians in 1964. According to Father Riquet, there are two million Lebanese emigrants in America, Africa and Australia, three-quarters of whom are said to be Maronites. Many Lebanese living abroad still have Lebanese citizenship and therefore retain the right to vote in elections in their home-country.

Yet it is possible that among the Lebanese who were permanent residents in Lebanon in the 1960s, the Muslims and Druzes together would have outnumbered the Christians. The Christians would then still be the largest population group holding Lebanese citizenship, even when not counting the Lebanese living abroad, because the Druzes—said to number 6 per cent of the total population—are not Muslim.

3. In Lebanon before the civil war, wealth and poverty followed no ethnic pattern. The millionaire class included Muslims as well as Druzes and Christians. Great wealth also accumulated among the political leadership of the Palestinian refugees in the country. Those who lived in extreme poverty were, above all, the migrant workers from neighbouring Arab countries who had entered the country illegally and were earning their living without official permission. But the class living in misery and despair also included many Lebanese peasants from the south who had been forced to flee as the result of Palestinian guerrilla attacks on Israel and Israeli counter-attacks on Southern Lebanon. The Palestinian refugees who have lived in the country since 1948 have been supplied with food by the United Nations relief organisation, UNRWA. The Lebanese refugees who had been driven out of Southern Lebanon by the Palestinian guerrilla war, on the other hand, were assisted by no international relief organisation.

4. While heavy fighting was going on in Lebanon, not even a

start was made in forming an administration for a separate
Christian state in the area defended by the Christian militia.
On the other hand, the Lebanese who were supporting the
Palestinian guerrillas established a 'local administration' for
the predominantly Muslim- and Druze-inhabited Southern
Lebanon in the summer of 1976. At the head of it was the
Druze leader Kemal Jumblatt. Neither the Christians nor the
Muslims of Lebanon wanted the country to be divided.

5. The propaganda, which the Palestinians initiated, accusing
the Lebanese Christians of fighting under the Cross and thus
perverting Christian values, was especially effective in the
West. This particular accusation was spread in Europe also
by some Greek Orthodox Christians of the Patriarchate of
Antioch, because an important part of the higher clergy of
the Patriarchate sympathised with the radical Lebanese Left
in the civil war. For many years the Patriarch of Antioch has
kept in close contact with Moscow. But the militia of the
Lebanese Christians fought their defensive war not in the
name of Christendom but as the 'Lebanese Front'. They were
fighting for the independence of their homeland. The Cross
was indeed worn by many Lebanese Christians but not as a
military emblem; and they had not the remotest intention of
converting Muslims and Druzes to Christianity. For
Lebanese mountain peasants whose homelands have never
been subject to Islam, the Cross symbolised freedom of belief.
Even today, Lebanese Christians have not forgotten that in
the Ottoman Empire the *dhimmis*, who were protected
Christians subjects, were forbidden by Islamic law from
wearing crosses publicly.

6. From the first weeks of the war, the Palestinian guerrillas
and the Lebanese Left systematically spread horror propaganda in the West about the Lebanese Christians. They
were supported by the information offices of the Palestine
Liberation Organisation in the West. Forged pictures were
passed to Western news agencies in Beirut and in Europe.
The Lebanese Maronite Patriarch, who was usually reserved
in his statements on political matters, warned against this
horror propaganda in a letter he sent to the permanent
conferences of Catholic bishops in many countries.

7. Arab Marxists have used 'Imperialism', 'Zionism' and
'Reaction' as fighting catchwords against various political
adversaries over the last two decades. Primitive though they

are, the words have a certain effect on the politically uneducated masses in the Arab countries. Especially suited to Arab psychology is the statement of the Arab Left that the Lebanese civil war was the result of a 'plot', hatched by the United States, Israel and Syria together. The romantic hypothesis of a secret plot against Lebanon in which the United States was the prime mover cannot be substantiated from a sober analysis of the active political forces in the country and the course of events. However, these slogans proved to be powerful political weapons.

POSTSCRIPT

In the politics of the Arab countries, the scenery often changes with an abruptness that bewilders the non-Arab observer. The deadly enemies of yesterday clasp each other today in a fraternal embrace; yet they are secretly preparing for a new conflict tomorrow. After a conference in the small East Lebanese town of Chtaura on 25 July at which representatives of the Lebanese and Syrian governments and the Palestine Liberation Organisation took part, the Palestinian guerrillas, in August 1977, surprisingly changed their attitude to their former enemies in the Lebanese civil war. After a visit to President Sarkis, the Palestinian leader Arafat explained that the guerillas wished to 'start a new chapter' in their relations with the Lebanese Christians.

Sarkis's predecessor, President Franjiya, whom the Palestinians had labelled a separatist, a reactionary and a plain criminal during the war, was suddenly praised by Arafat as a true friend of the Palestinians.

Should this declaration be taken to mean that the leaders of the Palestinian guerrillas had recognised their errors and were prepared, in a spirit of contrition, to adopt a policy of sincere reconciliation with the Lebanese Christians? The contrary was rather to be feared. The Palestinians have recognised that they needed a breathing space in order to stand their ground in Lebanon against the Christians. Their declarations after the Chtaura meeting gave an impression of total insincerity that was positively comic, and only one conclusion was to be drawn from it: the Palestinians were preparing a new attack. Indeed, early in September Palestinian guerrillas resumed their attacks on Christian villages in South Lebanon. This time the Syrian forces in Lebanon were in open support of the Palestinians, while Israeli artillery protected the Christian villages near the Israeli-Lebanese border. By late September the fighting in South Lebanon had diminished considerably in scale, in the weeks that followed a new rapprochement between the Palestinian guerrilla movement and the Syrian Government emerged, representing a major political trend in the Near East. The principal reason for this surprising development appears to have been the ruthless Soviet pressure applied to both the Syrian Government and the Palestinian leaders.

The attitude of the Lebanese Christians remained unchanged throughout 1977. It was not always easy, however, to analyse their point of view, since certain of their traditional leaders like Pierre Gemayel—the aged founder of the Kataeb Party— began, once again, to use the habitual euphemisms of Near Eastern politics and talk about 'brotherly relations' between the Christians of Lebanon and all Arab states, while countries like Iraq, Libya and Kuwait continued to show open hostility towards the political aspirations of the Christian population in Lebanon.

Beshir Gemayel, the youngest son of Pierre Gemayel, who in 1976 was appointed Commander-in-Chief of the 'Lebanese Forces'—the joint forces of all Christian militias in Lebanon— uses more convincing language. He has made it perfectly clear that the younger generation of Lebanese Christians want to survive as independent human beings and as Christians in a free democratic state, not as subjects, as *dhimmis*, under Islamic rule or as third-class citizens in a Communist 'people's democracy' ruled by Palestinians, Syrians or the radical Lebanese Left. The determination of the young Lebanese Christians to defend their freedom and their Christian values gives them considerable political strength in their difficult struggle for survival.

APPENDIXES

I

THE MILITARY FORCES ENGAGED IN
THE LEBANESE WAR (NOVEMBER 1976)

1. *The Peace Force*

Since the Cairo Conference of Arab heads of states (25 and 26 October 1976), the following units have belonged to the peace force of the Arab League:

(*a*) Syrian troops in Lebanon, said to number more than 20,000 men;

(*b*) The peace troops of Saudi Arabia, Libya and Sudan, which were sent to Lebanon as early as summer 1976. They numbered no more than 3,000 men in 1976. The Libyans left the country during the winter of 1976–7.

The peace force was strengthened by additional units from North and South Yemen, from the United Arab Emirates and from the Sudan. Their first military commander was the Lebanese colonel Ahmad al Hajj. The Lebanese President Elias Sarkis is politically responsible for their operations, and he is assisted by a group of senior Lebanese officers who remained neutral during the civil war.

2. *The 'Lebanese Forces' (fighting units of the Lebanese Christians)*

(*a*) Second only to the Syrian peace troops, the militia of the Kataeb Party is the strongest military power in Lebanon. The commander of the militia, as well as the supreme commander of the Unified Command of the 'Lebanese Forces', the united militias of Lebanese Christians, is Beshir Gemayel, a son of Pierre Gemayel, founder and leader of the Kataeb Party.

(*b*) The National Liberal Party of the former Christian President Camille Chamoun maintains an élite militia called *Numur* (a plural formation of an Arab word, meaning 'the tigers'; sing. *nimr*, 'tiger') and a numerically larger unit called *'Ahrar'* (the 'Free' or the 'Liberals'). Both *Numur* and *Ahrar* are under the command of Dani Chamoun, a son of the party leader Camille Chamoun.

(*c*) In North Lebanon, Christian leaders have united their followers into one common militia, called *Marada*. This home guard derives its name from the mountain tribe of the Maradites who, during the Islamic conquest of Syria, fiercely resisted the Arabs. The Arabic root of the word also contains a reference to rebellion, so that the *Maradas* also render their name as 'revolutionaries' or 'rebels'. Their military leader is Toni Franjiya, son of the former Lebanese President Suleiman Franjiya.

(*d*) Since the autumn of 1976, a militia called 'Army for the Liberation of the South', consisting of Lebanese Christians, has been fighting in South Lebanon under the command of Colonel Saad Haddad.

(*e*) During the war, the Christian Lebanese organisation *'Tanzim'* (the Arabic word means 'reform' or simply 'organisation') maintained its own effective militia. At times it was mistakenly identified with other organisations. *Tanzim* was founded in 1968 as a secret organisation with the name 'Movement of the Cedars' (*Mouvement des Cèdres,* Arabic *harakat al arz*). At times it was also known by the name 'League' (*al-rabita*'). The name 'Movement of the Cedars' caused the organisation to be confused later with the fighting organisation 'Guardians of the Cedars', and the name 'League' led to a further mistaken identification, namely with the 'Maronite League'. Consequently the secret organisation which emerged from the 'Movement of the Cedars' has, since 1975, only been known by the name *'Tanzim'*. *Tanzim* had no party leader, but only a military high command. Its official spokesmen were the Lebanese physician Fuad Shemali and the military leader of the militia, George Adwan.

(*f*) The 'Guardians of the Cedars' (*hurras al arz*) have taken over their ideology from the Lebanese poet Said Aql, born in 1912. Cedar trees are the symbol of the Lebanese state, and a green cedar has been incorporated into the national flag. But the cedar is also a symbol of the Christian traditions of the country. The Guardians of the Cedars declare that the Lebanese are not Arabs, but a people on their own. Spokesmen of the Guardians of the Cedars have declared that they are determined to fight until the last Palestinian has left Lebanon. The leader of this small militia is Major Etienne Saqr, known by the pseudonym 'Abu Arz'. In the West, the 'Guardians of the Cedars' are often mistaken for the 'Maronite League' of the attorney Shakir Abu Suleiman, a movement which does not control a militia. The 'Maronite League' stands for the political interests of the Maronite religious community in Lebanon.

(*g*) Under the leadership of Colonel Antoine Barakat, a section of the former Lebanese army joined the militia of the Christians. Other smaller army units joined various Christian militia organisations as separate fighting units, although these do not recognise Barakat as their leader.

3. *Palestinian opponents of the Lebanese Christians*

(*a*) The largest Palestinian fighting organisation is the guerrilla organisation al-Fatah. It receives arms from the Soviet Union and from several Arab countries. A Palestinian, known by the pseudonym 'Abu Jihad', was in 1976 responsible for military operations in Lebanon.

(*b*) During the civil war, the 'Democratic Popular Front for the Liberation of Palestine' became the second largest Palestinian fighting organisation in Lebanon. The leader of this guerrilla organisation is the East Jordanian Christian Nayef Hawatmeh, who is also the most lucid exponent of Marxist ideology within the Palestinian guerrilla movement.

(*c*) The 'Popular Front for the Liberation of Palestine', founded by the Palestinian paediatrician George Habash, specialised at one time in hijacking aeroplanes and carrying out kidnappings in Western countries. It participated in the fighting in Lebanon only with guerrilla units of limited strenth, but it played an important political role as a radical Marxist force during the war.

(*d*) The Palestinian guerrilla organisation known as 'Popular Front for the Liberation of Palestine—General Command' split in the late summer of 1976 into two wings—one pro-Syrian and the other anti-Syrian. Since then this guerrilla organisation has scarcely played any role in the civil war.

(*e*) Units of the 'Palestine Liberation Army', which had once been stationed in Egypt, were sent to Lebanon during the summer of 1976. There, under the leadership of Egyptian officers, they fought side by side with Fatah guerrillas.

4. *The 'National Movement' or 'National Front': Left- and Right-wing Lebanese Radicals*

The Lebanese opponents of the Christian militias have joined together in the 'National Movement', a collective name given to a variety of groups. In the West these political groups are frequently referred to as 'Left-Wing Muslims', but this label is misleading in several ways. First of all, the spokesman for the 'National Movement' during the war, Kemal Jumblatt, was no Muslim but belonged to the post-Islamic secret sect of the Druzes. Numerous followers of the organisations which joined together in the 'National Movement' were neither Muslims nor Druzes but Christians, mostly belonging to the Greek Orthodox Church. The strongest fighting unit within the 'National Movement' is the militia of the Lebanese 'National Socialists', which is not Left-wing, but a radical fascist organisation of the Right. At the end of 1976, the 'National Movement' comprised the following militia and fighting units:

(*a*) The party of the Lebanese 'National Socialists' (P.P.S.), which already had a powerful militia before the civil war. After the Fatah guerrillas, these fascists are the most important opponents of the Christians. The main body of the party, under the leadership of the Greek Orthodox Christian Inaam Raad, belongs to the 'National Movement'. Some splinter groups are opposing his leadership.
(*b*) The 'Progressive Socialist Party', founded by the Marxist Druze leader Jumblatt, was made up of armed Druze peasants from the central plateau of Lebanon. These peasants recognised their feudal lord both as military leader and as head of their party. Outside the Druze territory the party has little influence and controls only weak fighting units.
(*c*) The 'Lebanese Communist Party', which is supported by a number of Christians, also has its own militia. The general secretary of this pro-Soviet Communist party is the Greek Orthodox Christian Nikola Shawi.
(*d*) The 'Independent Nasserite Movement' stands for Arab nationalism and is especially strong among the Sunni Muslims in Beirut. Its militia called itself '*Murabitun*'. The leader of the party, Ibrahim Koleilat, who operated during the civil war under the pseudonym 'Abu Shakir', received arms and money for his militia from Libya and Iraq.
(*e*) The 'Movement of 24 October' is a Marxist organisation in the North Lebanese port of Tripoli. Its political and military leader is Farouk Makaddam. Its membership consists predominantly of Sunni Muslims. The organisation co-operates in Tripoli closely with some Leftist radical groups of Armenian and Greek Orthodox Christians and with the Lebanese branch of the pro-Soviet Iraq Baath party whose leader Abdul Majeed al Raffi was elected in 1972 as a member of the Beirut parliament.
(*f*) During the first winter of the civil war, the Muslim wing of the Lebanese armed forces split off under the rebel Lieutenant Ahmad Khatib and formed the 'Arab Army of Lebanon'. At first the followers of Ahmad Khatib threatened the Christian rural towns and villages in East Lebanon, but then withdrew to West Beirut.

5. *Lebanese organisations which maintain friendly links with Syria*

In June 1976 the Fatah guerrillas and the 'National Movement' disarmed the political friends of Syria in those regions of Lebanon which they controlled (mainly West Beirut and South Lebanon) But their organisation exerted considerable influence in those parts of East Lebanon, which were under the control of the Syrian troops There the pro-Syrian wing of the Arab Baath party is active under its Lebanese general secretary Assem Qanso.

(*a*) '*Saiqa*' (Thunder), the largest guerrilla organisation after al Fatah, stands close to the Syrian Baath party. *Saiqa* is led by the Palestinian Zuheir Muhsin.

(*b*) The 'Nasserite Organisation', a rival of the 'Independent Nasserites' who are allied with the Fatah guerrillas, seek to work out an Arab socialism which is independent of the socialism of both the East and the West. It draws most of its followers from among the Sunni Muslims in Beirut. During the summer of 1976, its leader Kemal Shatila was for a time prisoner of the Fatah guerrillas in West Beirut.

(*c*) During the summer of 1976, the 'Kurdish Progressive Party' known in Beirut as '*Raz Kaari*' and led by Faisal Fakhru, as well as

(*d*) the 'Union of Lebanese Communists' (a party which is friendly towards the government of Syria), led by Nakhle Matran, maintained fighting units in Beirut.

(*e*) During the first months of the civil war, the Christian militias were also engaged in action by the 'Movement of the Deprived', which was led by Shiite *Imam* Musa Sadr. However, since the summer of 1976 this spiritual leader of the Shiite Muslims in Lebanon has taken up an ambivalent attitude in the civil war, and fluctuates between a pro-Syrian and a neutral position.

II
BIBLIOGRAPHICAL NOTE

Many Lebanese hoped that the world would understand their problems better once the fighting was over, but they were to be disappointed again. The censorship introduced by the Sarkis administration unduly favoured the Palestinian guerrillas. The Palestinian news agency WAFA was allowed to report freely from Beirut the views of the Palestine Liberation Organisation (P.L.O.). The Christian 'Lebanese Front', on the other hand, had no such free outlet to pass uncensored press information to the outside world. The Sarkis administration even threatened to close the small Christian radio station *Saut Lubnan* ('Voice of Lebanon'), while several Palestinian stations continued to work illegally from Lebanese territory.

Because of censorship by the Government, the war diaries of Camille Chamoun, the most prominent Lebanese leader and a former head of state, had to be printed secretly. The first edition of this work, *Crise au Liban* ('Crisis in Lebanon'), covering events from January 1976 until the arrival of Syrian troops in Beirut, gives no indication of either the publisher or the printer.

Chamoun's *Crise au Liban* was stilly being sold in Beirut at the end of 1977. But the book next to it in documentary importance—*Le Livre Blanc Libanais: documents diplomatiques 1975–76* (Beirut 1976)—is very hard to obtain. The official publication of the Lebanese Ministry of Foreign Affairs contains some of the most important diplomatic despatches and memoranda concerning the crisis, some in French but most in Arabic.

After the end of the fighting in Beirut, some large collections of material on the war were published in Arabic, for example *Hawadith Lubnan 1975–76* by Antoine Khoueiry, in three volumes, a *rudes indigestaque moles* of reports published previously by Arabic newspapers and various radio stations. The Sayyad newspaper group printed a similar work, *Wathiqat harb Lubnan* (Beirut 1977), of which only the first volume is known to the present author.

During the war, a group of Christian intellectuals met at the University of the Holy Spirit-Kaslik in Jouniyeh and published seven pamphlets in French and twenty in Arabic. The most important are: *Témoignages vivants sur la crise qui traverse le Liban* (No. 1, 1975, 29 pp., anonymous) and *Génocide au Liban* (No. 7, July 1976, 60 pp., anonymous).

The main arguments of official Palestinian propaganda on the Lebanese war are clearly set out in Said Haddad et Mourad Saleh, *Le Liban: chronique et analyse de la guerre civile* (Département de l'information et de l'orientation nationale de l'O.L.P., Paris 1976).

The book by the Lebanese historian Kamal S. Salibi, *Cross Roads to Civil War*, published in New York, London and Beirut, reflects some of the principal arguments of the P.L.O. and of the Lebanese Left. The book was written in the western sector of Beirut which was controlled by the Palestinians, and deals with events up to February 1976.

A book expressing the point of view of one of the intellectual leaders of the Lebanese Christians, Joseph Mouwanes of the University of the Holy Spirit-Kaslik—*Les Eléments structuraux de la personalité Libanaise* (Beirut 1973)—has become very rare since, during the early months of the war, crowds of Leftist demonstrators burned all copies on which they could lay their hands in Beirut. It is also difficult today to obtain copies of Charles Corm, *La montagne inspirée* (2nd edition, Beirut 1964). This great poem, which its Lebanese French-language author characterises as *chansons de geste*, is the key literary document of those Lebanese Christians who no longer wish to be called 'Arabs', but insist on the specific Lebanese cultural mission to the Mediterranean world.

As for general works on Lebanon, the *Area Handbook for Lebanon*, published by the U.S. Government Printing Office, Washington D.C., in 1969, and the volume of the *Guides bleus, Liban* (last available edition, Paris 1975) contain useful bibliographical notes.

INDEX

Aden, 33
Adwan, George, 72
Africa, Lebanese in, 17, 65
Ahrar militia, 71
Ahdab, Gen. Aziz al, 44, 61
Ain Rummaneh, viii, 39
al-Fatah, *see* Fatah
Aley, 23, 48
America, North and South, Lebanese in, 15, 33, 65
Amoun, Fuad, 20
Antioch, Greek Orthodox patriarch of, 66
Aql, Said, 72
Arab League, 45–6, 48
Arabic language, vii, viii, 4
Arafat, Yassir, 48, 49, 56, 60, 68
Aramco, 35
Armenians, 4, 6, 74
'Army for the Liberation of Occupied South Lebanon', 50
Arslan, 29
Ashrafiya, 41, 43
Assad, President, of Syria, 34; and peace efforts, 44

Baath Arab Socialist Party, vii, 34, 74, 75
Baidas, Yusuf, 35
Barakat, Col. A. 72
Beirut: ix, 1, 5, 6, 30, 41, 50, 74, 77; airport, 35, 45, 51, 56, 59; fighting in, 43, 57; division caused by war, 46–7, 53; centre occupied by Syria, 51
Bekaa valley, 1, 2, 3, 6, 7, 20, 44, 47
Beshir II, Druze Emir, 9, 11
'Black September', 42
Bustani, Gen., 36

Cabinet, distribution of seats, 52
'Cairo agreement' of Arab heads of state (1969), 36, 49, 60; broken by Palestinians, 37, 38
Cairo conference (1976), 49
Cedars, Guardians of the, 72
Censorship, 53, 57, 76; of foreign correspondents, 62–3
Census (1932), 15
Chamoun, Camille, President: 19, 27, 30, 46, 62, 71; criticism of Sarkis administration, 55; appointed foreign minister but boycotted, 62; war diaries, 76
Chamoun, Dani, 71
Chehab, Gen. Fuad, President, 19, 20, 23, 55
Christians, Lebanese: as new political force, vii; attitude to language, viii; emigrants, 15; position in state, 17–18; militias, 38, 43–4, 50, 51; besieged in East Lebanon, 45; and post-war reforms, 54–5; massacres of on Jumblatt's death, 57; supposed motives for fighting, 63ff.
Chtaura, 47, 48, 68
citizenship and right to vote, 17
Communist Party of Lebanon, 30, 74
Communist states, lack of support for UNWRA, 31
Coptic Christians, 17
Corm, Charles, 77

Damascus, 1, 5, 6, 20, 43
Dastur bloc, 24; Party, 28
De Gaulle, Gen., 11
Democratic Popular Front for the Liberation of Palestine, 34, 73

78

Dhimmis, 13, 69
Druze faith, Druzes: 4, 6, 7–8, 9, 10, 13–14, 15, 18, 23, 52, 54–5, 65; massacres of Christians (1859) 10, (after Jumblatt's death) 57

Eddé, Emile, 26
Eddé, Pierre, 27
Eddé, Raymond, 21, 27, 45
Education, Ministry of, 18
Egypt: 15, 17, 19–20, 31, 38; pro-Soviet policy, 21; as peace guarantor, 58
European Economic Community, 61–2
Faisal, Hashemite Emir, 10–11
Fakhreddin II, Druze Emir, 7–8, 11, 28
Fakhru, Feisal, 75
'Falange', ix, 24
Fatah, al- (Palestinian organisation), viii, 33, 37, 41, 59, 73; growth in prestige, 33
France, 10, 14, 31; mandate over Syria and Lebanon, 11, 29
Franjiya, Hamid, 20
Franjiya, Suleiman, President, 20, 29, 44, 46–7, 61, 68

Gaza Strip, 31, 51
Gemayel, Beshir, 43, 69, 71
Gemayel, Pierre, 20, 21, 26, 28, 39, 43, 69
Geneva conference, 51
Germany (West), ix, 31, 62
Great Britain, 10; mandate in Palestine, 31
Greek Catholics, *see* Melkites
Greek Orthodox Christians, 4, 9, 23, 73; patriarch, 13
Gregorian Orthodox, *see* Armenians

Habash, Dr George, 33–4, 59, 73
Haddad, Col. Saad, 72, 77
Hajj, Gen. Ahmed al, 50, 52, 71
Hakim, Adnan al, 24, 28
Hamade, Sabri, 20
Hammudeh, Yahya, 33
Haret Hureek, 43

hashish, production, 20
Hawatmeh, Nayef, 73
Hayat, Al, 21
Hélou, Charles, President, 21, 36
Hoss, Salim al, prime minister, 52, 53, 55, 57
Hussein, King, of Jordan, 37

Intra Bank, 35
Iraq: vii, 17, 21, 34, 69; support of Palestinian guerrillas, 38, 41, 58, 59, 74
Israel: vii, viii, 38; and United Nations, 31; withdrawal from Suez Canal, 42; wars with Arabs, *see* Wars; al-Fatah struggle with, 33; raids on Lebanon, 35–6, 37, 65; support for Lebanese Christian militias, 50, 58, 68; in Palestinian war propaganda, 64

Jews in Lebanon, 8, 13
Jisr al Basha camp, viii, 43, 46
Jordan, 1, 19, 32, 34, 47; civil war (1970), 37
Jouniyeh, 1, 47, 61
Jubail, 1, 27
Jumblatt, Kemal, Druze leader: ix, 20, 21, 24, 41, 43, 59, 66, 73; and 'Progressive Socialist Party', 28–9; murdered, 57

Karame, Rashid, prime minister, 20, 42, 62; support for Nasser, 22, 23; opposition to Pres. Hélou, 36
Karantina, 43
Kataeb Party, 20, 21, 24, 53; militia, 26, 27, 39, 41, 69, 71
Kfur, temporary seat of government, 61
Khalaf, Salah, viii
Khalid, King, of Saudi Arabia, 48
Khatib, Lieut. Ahmad, 44, 45, 74
Khoueiry, Antoine, 76
Khoury, Beshara al, President, 11, 14, 19, 28
Kissinger, Dr. H., 38, 41, 43
Koleilat, Ibrahim ('Abu Shakir'), 74

Kurdish Progressive Party, 75
Kurds, 17, 28
Kuwait: 33, 48, 56, 59, 69; support for Palestinians, 60; as peace guarantor, 58; Palestinians in, 59

language questions, vii, viii
Lebanese army, 41, 49
'Lebanese Front' (Christian), 54, 55, 60, 64
Left, Lebanese, 28, 30, 54, 63–4, 69; Christian membership, 52; alliance with Palestinian guerrillas, 43, 53, 66; militias, 26, 44
Libya: vii, 69; support for Palestinian guerrillas, 38, 41, 58, 59, 74; and peace force, 50, 71
literacy, 18

Marada militia, 71–2
Maron, John, 4–5
Maron, St., 4, 5
Maronite Christians, Church: 4, 5, 6, 9, 11, 13, 17, 23, 26, 27, 63, 65; among Palestine refugees, 35; murder and kidnapping of in war, 42
'Maronite League', 72
marriage laws, 54
Marxist ideology, 34, 73
'Melkart Agreement', 37, 39
Melkites, 4, 5–6, 13, 18
Meloy, U.S. ambassador, 61
Metni, Nassib, 20
Me'ushi, Maronite patriarch, 20, 21
Mouwanes, Joseph, 77
'Movement of Arab Nationalists', 33
Mruwweh, Kamil, 21
Muhsin, Zuheir, 34
Mukaddam, Farouk, 74
'Murabitun', 42, 62, 74
Muslims, Lebanese, in general: 12–14, 15, 52; drop demands for reform, 43–5; *and see* Shiite, Sunni Muslims

Nahj Bloc 23
Najjadeh Party, 28

Nasser, Abdul, President of Egypt, and followers: 19, 20, 23, 26, 29, 32, 55; 'Nasserite Organisation', 75
'National Bloc', 24, 26, 27
National-Liberal Party, 27, 39, 53, 64, 71; militia, 41
'National Movement' of Left, 57, 73
'National Pact' between communities (1943), 14, 17
National Socialist Party ('Syrian'), 29–30, 41, 46, 64, 73–4
Numur (Tigers) militia, 27, 71

Ottoman empire, 9; non-Islamic communities under, 13–14; *and see* Turkey

'Palestine Liberation Army', 44, 45
Palestine Liberation Organisation, 36, 68; founded, 32; *and see* Arafat, Palestinians
Palestinians: 27, 32; guerrillas, viii, 26, 35, 39, 44, 48, 50; propaganda, ix, 63–4, 66–7; refugees in Lebanon, 17, 31ff., 51, 65; armed refugee camps, 36, 38, 56, 59; high command, 37; relations of guerrillas with Lebanese state, 36–8, 48ff.
Pan-Arabism, vii, 28, 29
Papal Nuncio, 61
Parliament, 17, 23, 24; distribution of seats, 15ff., 25, 44
Peace Force, pan-Arab: 49, 52, 55–6, 57–8. 71; Syrians in, 50–2, 59, 71
Phoenician heritage, 1–2
Popular Front for the Liberation of Palestine, 33–4, 59, 73
President, office of, 14, 17
Progressive Socialist Party, 28–9

Qanso, Assem, 75

Raad, Inaam, 30, 74
Raffi, Abdul Majeed al, 74
Rashaya prisoners, 11
Refugees, *see* Palestinians
'Refusal Front', 59, 60

Riad, Mahmoud, 41

Riquet, Fr. Michel, 65

Riyadh conference and agreement: 48–9, 56; Palestinians breach of, 59

Russian (and U.S.S.R.) Orthodox Church, 5

Saab, Edouard, 63

Saade, Antoun, 29, 30

Sadat, President, of Egypt, suggests Lebanese peace plan, 48–9

Sadr, *Imam* Musa, 41, 64, 75

Saiqa organisation, 34, 59, 60

Salaam, Saab, 20

Saleh, Mourad, 77

Salibi, Kamal S., 77

Saqr, Major E., 72

Sarkis, Elias: ix, 27, 52, 71, 76; elected President, 45; negotiations with Palestinians, 48; policy of balance, 55

Saudi Arabia: 32, 33, 56, 59; and pan-Arab peace force, 49, 71; as peace guarantors, 58

Shatila, Kamal, 75

Shawi, Nikola, 74

Shiite Muslims, 4, 5–6, 14, 18, 20, 64, 75

Shikka, 47

Shouf Province, 6, 57

Shukairi, Ahmed, 22, 32, 33, 34

Sidon, 1, 6, 10, 37, 51

Soldatov, Soviet ambassador, 43

Solh, Riad al, 11, 14, 19

Somalia, vii

Soviet Union: 19, 20; foreign policy under Khrushchev, 19; and Palestinian guerrillas, 38, 41, 58, 69; embassy in Lebanon, 61

Sudan, and pan-Arab peace force, 49, 71

Suleiman, Shakir Abu, 72

Sunni Muslims, ix, 4, 6, 14, 18, 20, 28, 74, 75

Sweden, 20

Syria: vii, 1, 5, 19–20, 33, 56, 64; guest-workers in Lebanon, 17; support for Palestinian guerrillas, 38; political influence in Lebanon,

42, asked by Lebanon for military protection, 45; troops in Lebanon, 45–7, 48, 50–2, 58, 59; as peace guarantors, 58; *and see* Peace Force

Syrian Catholics, 6

Syrian Orthodox, 6, 17

Taqla, Philippe, 46, 62

Tanzim militia, 41, 72

Tell Zaatar camp, vii, 39, 43, 46

'Third Force' in Lebanese war, 42

Thirion, Marc, 63

Tripoli (Northern Lebanon), 1, 5, 6, 10, 30, 46, 51, 74

Turkey, 9, 10, 17; *and see* Ottoman Empire

Tyre, 1, 6

United Arab Emirates, and pan-Arab peace force, 49, 50, 71

'United Arab Republic', 19–20, 55

United Nations Relief and Works Agency (UNWRA), 31, 35, 65

United States of America: 1, 41; Eisenhower Doctrine and Lebanese support, 19, 21; Near East Policy, 21, 43; and UNWRA, 31, 32; embassy in Lebanon, 61; evacuation of citizens, 62; in Palestinian war propaganda, 64

Universities: American (Beirut), 21; Holy Spirit-Kaslik, 76, 77; St. Joseph, 26

WAFA (Palestinian news agency), 76

Wars: Arab-Israeli (1948), 17, 19, 31, 35; Six-Day (1967), 22, 32, 34; world wars, and Lebanon, 10–11; Lebanese: beginning, 39ff., and *passim*

Yemen, and pan-Arab peace force 49, 71

Yugoslavia, 31

Zahle, 6, 10